Alessia Amighini

MONEY AND MIGHT

Along the Belt and Road Initiative

**Foreword by
Alicia García-Herrero**

Cover: Cristina Bernasconi, Milan
Typesetting: Laura Panigara, Cesano Boscone (MI)

Copyright © 2021 Bocconi University Press
EGEA S.p.A.

EGEA S.p.A.
Via Salasco, 5 - 20136 Milano
Tel. 02/5836.5751 – Fax 02/5836.5753
egea.edizioni@unibocconi.it – www.egeaeditore.it

All rights reserved, including but not limited to translation, total or partial adaptation, reproduction, and communication to the public by any means on any media (including microfilms, films, photocopies, electronic or digital media), as well as electronic information storage and retrieval systems. For more information or permission to use material from this text, see the website www.egeaeditore.it

Given the characteristics of Internet, the publisher is not responsible for any changes of address and contents of the websites mentioned.

First edition: June 2021

ISBN Domestic Edition   978-88-99902-84-1
ISBN International Edition   978-88-31322-12-6
ISBN Digital International Edition 978-88-31322-13-3
ISBN Digital Domestic Edition   978-88-238-8278-2

Table of Contents

Foreword, by *Alicia García-Herrero*   VII

Abbreviations   XI

Introduction   3

1   Finance at the Heart of the Belt and Road Initiative   9
     The New Silk Roads: the birth of an idea   10
     The logic behind the myth   14
     The five pillars of the BRI   20
     BRI: China's foreign policy shift   28
     Why financial cooperation is essential in the BRI   32
     2020, a turning point?   41

2   The Art of Finance, with Chinese Characteristics   45
     The renminbi's long march   46
     The renminbi: an "unfinished" currency?   59
     The long hand of Chinese foreign loans   62
     China's financial outposts in the world   68
     Hong Kong: still a financial firewall for China?   75
     The e-RMB: China's great financial leap into the 21st century   85

3   The Renminbi as an Instrument of Soft Power   91
     The use of the renminbi as an international invoicing currency   92
     The renminbi in commodities trading   95
     Towards a "renminbi bloc"?   104
     The expansion of the renminbi in Europe   108

China's lending abroad: sovereign on market terms ... 116
Towards a new debt crisis with Chinese characteristics? ... 118
What are the prospects for the internationalisation
 of the renminbi? ... 123

Bibliography ... 127

Foreword

by *Alicia García-Herrero*[*]

The Belt and Road Initiative (BRI) has been widely analyzed by Chinese and international scholars, but less attention has been put to its financial implications. This book by Alessia Amighini is the best piece of work I have read so far that sheds some light on this topic. In fact, the author offers a very comprehensive view of the link between the BRI, as Xi Jinping's landmark project to enhance China's soft power, and the internationalization of the renminbi.

The importance of renminbi internationalization for China's rise cannot be underestimated. No hegemon has ever been dependent on the currency issued by the previous hegemon and this is what China would need to end up doing once its GDP surpasses that of the US, which – based on existing growth projections – is bound to happen as early as 2028. In fact, only about 2% of global transactions are denominated in RMB, as opposed to almost 40% in USD. In the same vein, only 2% of global foreign exchange reserves are denominated in RMB, versus over 60% in USD. In other words, China is an economic giant but with a weak currency, in terms of international use.

There are two sets of reasons why this is the case. The first is the size and liquidity of China's financial system. Actually, China's financial system used to be relatively small for the size of its economy, but that reality has changed rapidly since 2008 as banks' balance sheets grew sharply and so did the bond and the stock market. However, liquidity is still

---

[*] Alicia Garcia-Herrero is a Spanish economist and academic who has been the chief economist for Asia-Pacific at French investment bank Natixis since June 2015.

not as ample as that of the US financial markets, in fact far from that. Secondly, China's currency is not yet convertible since controls remain on China's financial account, especially as regards outflows, both of foreign direct investment and even more so of portfolio flows. While the process of China's financial opening has been accelerating in recent years, it remains asymmetrical as most of the developments still concentrate in attracting inflows.

China, being fully aware of the potential costs of opening up the financial account too quickly, is trying to square the circle with two main proposals. The first is financing projects along the BRI geographies, using renminbi as funding currency. This book deals with this issue at great length, which makes it an invaluable source of information as to how China is pushing the use of its currency and, more generally, renminbi internationalization.

The second way in which China is pushing its currency is by introducing the first digital currency among major central banks in the world. Chinese policy makers are introducing the digital renminbi, not only for domestic reasons – as cash in circulation has shrunk dramatically due to the widespread application of digital payments – but also for external reason. A crucial one is to reduce China's dependence from the US dollar whether it is for funding or investment purposes. This is even more the case after Trump started a trade war on China, which spread to a tech war with the help of the extraterritoriality of the dollar. The possibility of a financial war is also brewing with the investment ban on Chinese military firms. In other words, the emergence of China's own digital currency comes at just the right time as China's first mover advantage for its digital currency to be used overseas could enhance the acceptance of the currency whether for funding or investment and, thereby, reduce China's dependence on the US dollar. The use of digital currency also offers a new way of capital control through the tracing of financial flows.

This book offers an excellent overview of where we stand in this process and, thereby, become an invaluable source of understanding of how far China is from becoming the world's hegemon. In fact, China's GDP size is one aspect of what is needed. Another key one is the use of the renminbi internationally. Both the BRI and the way it is funded, as well as the overseas use of China's digital currency are two important ways in which China can achieve that goal.

All in all, I cannot but recommend reading this thorough analysis by Alessia Amighini on a topic of enormous relevance, not only for China but for the world.

Abbreviations

ADB	Asian Development Bank
AIIB	Asian Infrastructure Investment Bank
ANSO	Alliance of International Science Organizations
APEC	Asia-Pacific Economic Cooperation
ASEAN	Association of Southeast Asian Nations
BIS	Bank for International Settlements
BoE	Bank of England
BRI	Belt and Road Initiative
BRICS	Brazil Russia India China South Africa
BRNN	Belt and Road News Network
CAS	Chinese Academy of Sciences
CBIRC	China Banking and Insurance Regulatory Commission
CBOT	Chicago Board of Trade
CEEC	Central and Eastern European Countries
CFFEX	China Financial Futures Exchange
CGN	China General Nuclear Power Corporation
CIBM	China Interbank Bond Market
CIPS	China International Payments System
CLII	China Life Insurance Indonesia
CMI	Chiang Mai Initiative
CNH	Chinese Yuán (offshore)
CNY	Chinese Yuán (onshore)
CPC	Communist Party of China
CRCC	China Railway Construction Corporation
CSRC	China Securities Regulatory Commission
DCE	Dalian Commodity Exchange
ECB	European Central Bank
EEU	Eurasian Economic Union

ESM	European Stability Mechanism
GBA	Greater Bay Area
HIPC	Heavily Indebted Poor Countries
HKMA	Hong Kong Monetary Authority
HSBC	Hong Kong & Shanghai Banking Corporation
ICBC	Industrial and Commercial Bank of China
IMF	International Monetary Fund
LIDC	Low Income Developing Countries
LME	London Metal Exchange
MENA	Middle East and North Africa
MOFCOM	Ministry of Commerce, PRC
MoU	Memorandum of Understanding
MDRI	Multilateral Debt Relief Initiative
MSR	Maritime Silk Road
NDRC	National Development and Reform Commission
NRGI	Natural Resource Governance Institute
NYMEX	New York Mercantile Exchange
OBOR	One Belt, One Road
PBoC	People's Bank of China
PLA	People's Liberation Army
PRC	People's Republic of China
RMB	renminbi
RQFII	RMB Qualified Foreign Institutional Investor
SAR	Special Administrative Region
SCO	Shanghai Cooperation Organization
SDR	Special Drawing Rights
SEHK	Hong Kong Stock Exchange
SHFE	Shanghai Futures Exchange
SOE	State-owned enterprises
SPR	Cross-Border Trade Settlement Pilot Project
SREB	Silk Road Economic Belt
SSE	Shanghai Stock Exchange
SWIFT	Society for Worldwide Interbank Financial Telecommunication
TPP	Trans-Pacific Partnership
ZCE	Zhengzhou Commodity Exchange

> *Accept my money, or die.*
> – Kublai Khan, XIII cent.

Currency scholars date the invention of the first banknote in history (engraved on buckskin) to 118 B.C. during the Huang Dynasty, and the first paper banknote to 806 A.D. during the Song Dynasty. However, it was at the Great Khan's state mint in the ancient city of Khanbaliq that a real process of banknote production can truly be said to have begun in the 13th century. We know from Marco Polo's accounts:

> that the bark of those mulberry trees whose leaves are used to feed the silkworms is stripped, and that the thin inner ring which lies between the coarser bark and the wood of the tree is obtained. This is soaked and then pounded in a mortar until it is reduced to a pulp, and made into paper, similar to cotton paper, but very black. When it is ready for use, it is cut into pieces of money of different sizes, almost square, but a little longer than they are wide [...]
> The currency of this paper money is authenticated with as much form and ceremony as if it were in fact of pure gold or silver; for each note a number of officers, specially appointed, not only sign their names, but also affix their seals; and when this has been duly done by all of them, the principal officer, appointed by his majesty, having dipped the royal seal entrusted to his custody in vermilion, stamps the piece of paper with it, so that the form of the seal dyed with vermilion remains impressed upon it, by which it receives full authenticity as a current coin, and the act of counterfeiting is punished as a capital offence. When thus coined in large quantities, this paper money is circulated throughout all parts of the dominions of the Great Khan; nor dare any one, at the risk of his life, refuse to accept it in payment. All his subjects receive it without

hesitation, because, wherever their business calls them, they can dispose of it again in the purchase of such goods as they may have occasion to buy, as pearls, jewels, gold, or silver. With it, in short, every article may be purchased [...] All his Majesty's armies are paid with this coin, which is as valuable to them as gold or silver. On this basis, it can certainly be said that the Great Khan possesses the largest treasury of any ruler in the universe. (taken from *The Travels of Marco Polo*, Book 2, Chapter 18)

Today, China's currency strategy is not dissimilar to that of Kublai Khan: the use of the renminbi in international electronic payment platforms and the launch of a digital sovereign currency are together the contemporary version of the ancient mulberry bark, the innovation at the origin of a radical progress that may change the course of history.

Introduction

During an official visit to Kazakhstan in September 2013, Chinese President Xi Jinping suggested an innovative model of regional economic cooperation to foster collaboration in countries along the ancient Silk Road. He called this idea the "New" Silk Road. A month later that same year, during his speech to the Indonesian parliament in Jakarta, Xi projected a New Maritime Silk Road as an extension of the land-based one, a likeness of the historic Maritime Silk Road linking China to the Mediterranean.

Since it was first announced, much has been written about the Belt and Road Initiative (BRI). The BRI, with its deliberately vague name, evocative of transport networks, was initially presented, and thus welcomed by most, as a major infrastructure investment program. The aim of the initiative was increasing connectivity between China and the entire Eurasian continent, in particular the areas most in need of transport links and infrastructure – i.e. the countries of Central Asia – with Europe as its westernmost frontier.

Already at that time, the Chinese government had been exhaustively explaining the idea behind the BRI, to clarify its characteristics, and the motivations behind the project and thus clear the field of certain interpretations that had immediately been put forward on the expansionist and paternalistic intent of the initiative, which many compared to a great Marshall Plan for Central Asia. Far beyond transport infrastructure, the BRI is an ambitious strategy to enhance connectivity between Asia and Europe by promoting five types of connectivity: not only physical, but also commercial, digital, financial and cultural. According to the main reference document drafted by the National Development and Reform Commission (NDRC) of the People's Republic of China (PRC), now known as the BRI White Paper (the full title is *Vision and Actions on*

Jointly Building the Silk Road Economic Belt and 21st Century Maritime Silk Road), the BRI is based on five pillars: policy coordination, infrastructure connectivity, increased trade, financial integration, and cultural exchanges. Since October 2016, the BRI has become a state objective of the PRC, fully incorporated into its Constitution, reflecting the enormous importance of the Initiative among the country's policy objectives.

The BRI has quickly become the focus of all Chinese economic diplomacy, if not Chinese diplomacy tout court. Its aim is to promote China's integration into the global economy along much deeper avenues than ever before, i.e. well beyond international trade and investment flows abroad. Although the Chinese government officially prefers to call it an Initiative, it should be seen as a genuine programme for opening up the country, developed in response to changing domestic and international circumstances. The Chinese government has built a colossal economic, institutional and political communication effort in support of the BRI, to dispel fears of possible Chinese expansionism, with language that is full of allusions to the common benefits the Initiative intends to bring to all its supporters. Today, more than a hundred countries and international organisations have officially supported the BRI through Memoranda of Understanding (MoUs) of great symbolic – perhaps more than operational – value.

***

In the proliferation of books and articles on the BRI, both academic and journalistic, the financial pillar of the Initiative has so far received little attention. This despite the fact that it is a central element of the Initiative and in some respects, as this book seeks to show, its ultimate objective. Various essays, mainly academic articles with a technical-financial slant, have been devoted to some specific elements of China's financial integration strategy with the rest of the world. By far the most prominent among them is the internationalisation of the renminbi, since 1969 the official name of the Chinese currency, which literally means "the people's currency" – from the Chinese *rén mín* (people), *bì* (currency). From this word comes the common abbreviation (RMB), although it does not conform to the ISO 4217 code officially used for national currencies (according to this international standard the three-letter code for the Chinese currency would be CNY, from the official name *Chinese yuán*).

The internationalisation of the renminbi is undoubtedly a much-studied topic as far as its characteristics and evolution, and has been part of China's strategy of integrating the country into the world economy since well before the BRI was conceived. There is no precise date that we can identify as the starting point of the somewhat ambiguous objective of internationalising the renminbi, but it has certainly been under discussion in China since at least early 2002. Initially a vague notion, the prospect took shape within a few years and in 2006 was outlined by a study group sponsored by the People's Bank of China (PBoC), the Chinese central bank, in the report that would become the turning point for the entire strategy (*The Timing, Path, and Strategies of RMB Internationalization*). It stated that the internationalisation of the renminbi would promote China's international status, competitiveness, and influence on the world economy, in part by enhancing the country's power (as an international currency issuer). Therefore, this step had become inevitable. In 2014, the inaugural year of the BRI, the renminbi's internationalisation process had already been in full swing for at least five years, if we count 2009 as the date when its use as a currency in international trade transactions began.

The BRI and the internationalisation of the renminbi are both strategies promoted by China in the 21st century to increase its integration into the world economy. They came about at different times and with parallel, if complementary, aims. Indeed, there is a great synergy between them. On the one hand, as we shall see in Chapter 1, greater international circulation of the renminbi is indispensable for the completion and smooth functioning of the BRI. The vast financial resources needed to implement BRI projects around the world cannot be denominated in renminbi (which has no real official circulation outside China), but require an international reference currency, mainly the dollar. Although China is still the world's leading country in terms of the amount of foreign exchange reserves (with $3,400 billion as of March 2020), one can hardly imagine it using these funds to finance long-term investment projects abroad. This has two implications. The first is that China alone cannot finance the BRI, but must channel extensive financial resources from a large number of countries. This was done through the establishment in late 2015 of a specially dedicated multilateral development bank, the Beijing-based Asian Infrastructure Investment Bank (AIIB). The second implication is the need for China to increase the RMB's circulation area in order to reduce its financial and political dependence on the dollar.

On the other hand, the BRI provides a formidable platform for pursuing an ingenious currency strategy of gradually incrementing the international circulation of the renminbi – as we shall see in Chapter 2. By intensifying Chinese trade and investment in partner countries, the BRI significantly increases demand for the renminbi outside China and thereby creates the conditions for extending its circulation well beyond its borders. The most interesting aspect of this strategy is the highly innovative and clever way in which China intends to circulate the renminbi around the world. This will be done not through a progressive and unconditional convertibility of the currency (as in past cases of internationalisation of non-convertible currencies, e.g. the Japanese yen or German mark), but through a system of controlled convertibility based on deposits of renminbi in a network of banks in various countries around the world. More recently, China has also issued a digital currency that can also be used in international payments.

As it becomes more widely circulated outside national borders, the "people's money" thus becomes an instrument and vehicle for China's growing power over its economic partners, as we shall see in Chapter 3. The latter, enticed and driven by the advantages stemming from maintaining good economic relations with the world's most dynamic market, are increasingly agreeing to subordinate political relations with China to economic relations with its large corporations and wealthy consumers. This has now also extended to accepting shares and securities denominated in renminbi. Beijing's ultimate goal is to create an international renminbi circulation area parallel to that of the dollar. The financial BRI is an international renminbi liquidity network that relies on foreign financial institutions operating bilaterally with Chinese counterparts, outside the PRC's borders, but within the PBoC's sphere of monetary sovereignty.

It is therefore clear that the financial BRI is distinguished by two related themes, both of which have been dealt with extensively in recent years. The first theme is the system of financial institutions (including the AIIB) that have been designed and set up to support BRI projects and that operate mainly in dollars. The second is the financial consequences of the BRI, i.e. the effects on the external accounts of countries receiving financing for Chinese infrastructure investment projects. Since the funding is provided on market terms, and often (so far overwhelmingly) to countries with low per capita incomes, some of which are already highly indebted, it risks leading many of these countries into a "debt trap," i.e. over-indebtedness to the rest of the world, and in particular to China. This creates not only financial and economic but often also political dependence, as the resulting power relations are heavily skewed in favour of the interests of the creditor, as we shall see in Chapter 3. In this way, Beijing hopes that the BRI will foster the emergence of a growing need for a China-centred international chain payments system, a system parallel to the dollar circulation area. This would also satisfy many of the aspirations associated with the internationalisation of the renminbi. From this perspective, the BRI can be seen as the vehicle for a Chinese strategy to set a new course in globalisation, aimed at achieving a multipolar system in which China has its own place and can continue to participate actively in the global economy while respecting its own rules.

***

This book is the fruit of many years of study and analysis on the path of international opening and integration that China has embarked on since the 1980s. Although the obvious geo-political significance of the BRI has attracted the attention of political observers and media coverage of the BRI is huge, there are comparatively few economic studies on the effects of this Initiative. Chinese scholars have studied the related banking, currency, financial and trade issues; explored the possibilities for agricultural and energy cooperation; and sought to address misunderstandings about the objectives of China's designs. For their part, foreign scholars have mainly analysed its effects on regional balances and international relations, but there are few in-depth analyses of the economic scope of the BRI. Although China has stated that the BRI has no political objectives, politics and economics are intimately intertwined, and finance is the real instrument for extending China's power to influence the world: national financial and monetary capabilities are aimed at achieving foreign policy objectives.

1 Finance at the Heart of the Belt and Road Initiative

The BRI is China's most important national development strategy of the 21st century. By significantly increasing connectivity between China and numerous countries in Asia, Europe, as well as Africa and the Middle East, it aims to create a broad, economically interdependent region in which China serves as the driving force and nerve centre. With the BRI, China pursues major internal economic objectives, among which, principally, rebalancing the enormous regional development gaps between coastal and internal provinces, gaps which emerged during the course of the Thirty Glorious Years (1980-2010) of very rapid economic growth. To an equally significant extent, China is searching for new outlet markets for the great productive overcapacity accumulated in those same years by the system of the great State enterprises.

But China alone cannot finance the BRI. In fact, huge financial resources are required to implement projects in numerous countries around the world. Consequently, at the end of 2015, China promoted the establishment of a new multilateral development bank, the aforementioned AIIB, based in Beijing. This bank now has over a hundred-member countries, with a total paid-up capital of over $100 billion. But an immense integrated economic area can only really function with a benchmark currency that is regularly accepted throughout the region, and this cannot be – in Beijing's eyes – a third-country currency, such as the dollar. This is why China needs to boost the international circulation of the renminbi, thereby reducing its dependence on the dollar, which is increasingly financial as well as political. Financial cooperation is therefore the lifeblood of the whole initiative.

The New Silk Roads: the birth of an idea

In October 2013, during a speech to the Indonesian parliament, as part of a visit to various Southeast Asian nations for a meeting of the Asia-Pacific Economic Cooperation (APEC) forum's economic leaders, Chinese President Xi Jinping proposed the idea of a new Silk Road. This initiative was inspired by the ancient Silk Road, which from Fujian, a south-eastern province of China facing the island of Taiwan, connected China with the Mediterranean Sea, through the South China Sea and across the Strait of Malacca, the Indian Ocean, to Europe. The ancient route was used by China to export silk, ceramics and tea and to connect the territories and peoples bordering the East China Sea, the Bay of Bengal and the Arabian Sea through trade.

The idea of rebuilding a network of links between China and Europe was initially presented by Xi as an ambitious infrastructure development programme (although the geographical confines had yet to be defined). The aim was improving the current inefficient Eurasian trade routes, through new connectivity networks in Central, West and South Asia, but also reaching out to the Middle East and East and North Africa. From simple initial ideas, over time the design of the BRI has been refined and today includes two distinct routes, crossing the land and the sea. The first is the Silk Road Economic Belt (SREB), which today comprises a series of corridors, six of which are currently being planned or built (the China-Mongolia-Russia corridor; the New Eurasian Land Bridge; the China-Central Asia-West Asia Corridor; the China-Pakistan Corridor; the Indochina Peninsula Corridor; the Bangladesh-China-India-Myanmar Corridor). The second maritime route is called the Maritime Silk Road (MSR). With these networks, China now intends to improve connectivity between Europe and Asia, through modern means of transport, in order to increase trade, investment and economic development. The Initiative also calls for the intensification of diplomatic relations, scientific progress and cultural exchanges between all countries and regions of the Eurasian continent.

Connections between major European and Asian civilisations began more than two thousand years ago, thanks to the bold and ambitious camel caravans that explored and opened what is now known as the ancient Silk Road. Today the new links and corridors (covering Central Asia, the Caucasus, the Black Sea and the Caspian Sea, the countries bordering the Mediterranean, the entire European Union in general, and the central-eastern part of the Baltic in particular) are included in the BRI as an attempt to revive the old ambition to integrate the Eurasian continent.

Soon after the initial references to the Initiative, the Chinese government not only gave it the name "New Silk Road," but chose an official Chinese name 一带一路 (*yī dài yī lù*), an expression that literally translates, "one belt, one road." Although the literal translations from Chinese are all rather obscure, this did not prevent the rapid spread in the West of the use of the official English term that the government had initially chosen, namely "One Belt, One Road" (hence the acronym OBOR). But later (as early as September 2015) the Chinese government changed the official English name of the initiative to "Belt and Road Initiative" (BRI). This alteration in the official English name (while keeping the same Chinese name) might seem to be just a minor adjustment of the official translation. But in fact, as Yuan Li (Li, 2017) suggests, it signals some political, historical and cultural concerns on the part of the Chinese government, the origin of which is very interesting to understand. Indeed, the name BRI is intended to depart from the two names initially used, each of which carried connotations that were extremely uncomfortable for the Chinese government.

First of all, OBOR distances itself from the idea of a new "Silk Road," an expression (from the German *Seidenstraße*) coined by the German geographer Ferdinand von Richthofen in 1877. To a certain extent, therefore, Germany and not the Chinese government is the holder of the intellectual property rights to the name "Silk Road." Moreover, the New Silk Road was already the name of an initiative launched by the United States in 2011 to connect Afghanistan and Central Asia, aimed at integrating the region and strengthening its potential as a transit area between Europe and East Asia. In addition, in the late 1990s, the Japanese government under Obuchi Keizo announced a "Silk Road Diplomacy" aimed at strengthening Japan's involvement in Central Asia. The Chinese version of the new Silk Road plan was going to be very different from the previous American and Japanese programmes, both of which had made little progress. Indeed, China's idea from the outset had been to design a platform for regional cooperation and integration, therefore names that created connotations with previous unilateral programmes were not appropriate. Hence the Chinese government decided to use a different name for the BRI initiative. The literal translation of the expression *yī dài yī lù* in English (One Belt, One Road) is also rather unfortunate: in English the structure "one..., one..." is usually used to emphasise the meaning of "each" or "the same," as in the phrase "one person, one vote" or "One World, One Dream," while in the original Chinese it is mainly used to refer to "abstract things." As reported by Li (2017), "both Chinese and foreign politicians, such as Fu Ying, deputy minister of China's Ministry of Foreign Affairs, and Kevin Rudd, former prime minister of Australia, have suggested using different English translations to refer to the initiative." Since its introduction in 2013, the initiative has also evolved very quickly, expanding from "one" belt and "one" road, to include "many belts" and "many roads." So for all these reasons, the official English name of the initiative was changed from OBOR to BRI.

Today, the BRI has a much broader scope than its predecessors, namely the ancient Silk Road dating back to the Han dynasty (206 B.C.-220 A.D.) and the opening-up policy known as "Going Out," launched by the Chinese government in 1999 to facilitate the expansion of Chinese enterprises abroad, of which the BRI can be considered an evolution. While the original Silk Road comprised land and sea routes linking Xi'an to Rome mainly through southern corridors, passing through Iran and Turkey, the BRI is expected to also pass through Central Asia, Russia and Eastern Europe and end in Rotterdam. Moreover, unlike the old Silk Road, which was largely an unplanned result of trade activities between China and its partner countries, the current project is a projection of a national development strategy outisde its own borders with a potentially strong impact on international development. Similarly, the Going Out policy aimed to increase and facilitate China's direct investment abroad, relying on the fact that host countries would welcome Chinese investors in the hope of indirectly benefiting from China's growth through increased Chinese demand for their manufactured goods or natural resources. That policy was supported by the China Development Bank and between 2000 and 2015 led to a more than tenfold increase in China's trade with natural resource-rich countries in Southeast Asia, Latin America and Africa.

Currently, the SREB is consistent with China's periphery policy since 1991. This is the year when the independence of the five Central Asian republics (Kazakhstan, Kyrgyzstan, Tajikistan, Turkmenistan and Uzbekistan) prompted China to adopt a political strategy (or periphery policy) aimed at exploring common ground with its new neighbours in both economic and security spheres, to develop good political and economic relations with them. Indeed, the five Central Asian republics, together with Russia, Mongolia, India, Pakistan, Afghanistan, Iran and Turkey, were from the outset the main countries to be involved in the SREB. Nevertheless, to this day the geography of the whole BRI remains a matter of debate and there are numerous unofficial maps showing the routes and paths of the New Silk Roads. In what is commonly known as the SREB and MSR White Paper, published in 2015, the Chinese government explicitly states that the SREB "is aimed at connecting China, Central Asia, Russia and Europe (on the Baltic side); connecting China with the Persian Gulf and the Mediterranean Sea through Central Asia and West Asia; and connecting China with Southeast Asia, South Asia and the Indian Ocean."

Geographically, the SREB (remember: the land part of the BRI) consists of three main routes. The first starts in China and runs through Central Asia and Russia to Europe via the Baltic Sea. The second starts in China and continues through Central Asia and West Asia to the Persian Gulf and the Mediterranean Sea. The third starts in China and crosses South-East Asia and South Asia to the Indian Ocean. The MSR (Maritime Silk Road) goes from China's coastal ports through the South China Sea to the Indian Ocean, extending to Africa and Europe. The Initiative reaches at least 60 countries, representing 64% of the world's population (4.4 billion people) and 30% of global GDP ($21 trillion). The areas covered by the BRI are mainly poor, developing regions, located between the East Asian and advanced European economies, across three continents, with enormous potential for economic development in the near future.

To realise this Initiative, China has concluded a series of State Agreements with several dozen countries since its inception, starting with Kazakhstan in December 2014, with which it signed an agreement on *Joint Construction of the Silk Road Economic Belt*. About five months later, China entered into an agreement with Russia entitled *Joint Declaration on Cooperation between the Construction of the Silk Road Economic Belt and the Eurasian Economic Union*, and with Uzbekistan an *Agreement on Expansion of Mutually Beneficial Trade and Economic Cooperation* under the framework of the SREB Initiative. In early 2016, Beijing and Cairo signed a *Memorandum of Understanding on a Joint Agreement on Promoting the Construction of the Silk Road Economic Belt and the 21st Century Maritime Silk Road*. All these agreements are very different from international treaties that have real legal force. In fact, as already mentioned, these accords take the form of understandings, usually of temporary duration, called Memoranda of Understanding for cooperation in the implementation of various aspects of the BRI within the territories of the signatory countries.

Over time, China's diplomatic efforts to broaden the range of BRI partner countries have intensified at a rapid pace, and there are now 138 countries that have signed such agreements. This intense diplomatic action has been accompanied by an equally energetic activity of state lending to a growing number of low- and middle-income countries, investment by Chinese companies abroad, and strengthening trade links with partner countries. All these efforts are signs of a marked change in China's international projection in the 21st century from the introverted attitude the country held throughout the 20th century.

The logic behind the myth

Far beyond the myth of its name, the BRI pursues multiple economic and political objectives. Since its announcement, the true aims of the BRI have been a hotly debated topic in academia, think tanks and the media. On the one hand, the official position presented by the Chinese authorities is that the BRI is primarily an economic initiative, focusing on mutually beneficial cooperation and the socio-economic advantages that the Initiative could bring to China and other participating countries. On the other hand, many have gone so far as to interpret the BRI as an overt, audacious Chinese expansion strategy with military and security aspirations. In this perspective, it was initially compared to the Marshall Plan and described as a threat to the international liberal order. There is a huge divergence between the great emphasis of Chinese propaganda on the shared benefits of the programme and the geostrategic perspective of those who read the Initiative in a totally conflicting way. Whatever the true geopolitical impact of the BRI, the fact that the Chinese government has claimed that it is an economic initiative with a political purpose requires careful analysis.

Although analyses of geopolitical perspectives on BRI objectives have contributed to a greater understanding of the Initiative in the years since its announcement, the interpretations offered usually focus only on specific aspects of the BRI. As the Initiative is multifaceted, reducing it to only one of its dimensions loses sight of the overall picture and the links between the different dimensions. In particular, modern international relations studies emphasise that theories of world politics should seek to consider the interaction between international and domestic dynamics.

A useful starting point for interpreting the deep motivations and objectives of the BRI is the attention the Chinese authorities pay to the dissemination activity on the subject, including the meticulous choice of terms allowed in the official narrative, as we have seen since the initial choice of the name. In terms of terminology, the tendency is for the BRI to be called a "strategy" at home and an "initiative" abroad. In the domestic narrative, the BRI has been included, since November 2013, in the Comprehensive Reform Project adopted by the Central Committee of the Chinese Communist Party (CCP) as a priority policy to be implemented by 2020. This is a genuine development strategy, which led to the State Council's approval of detailed plans for the BRI submitted by various government departments in March 2015. Since then, this undertaking has become a full-fledged state goal of the PRC.

International communication activity on the BRI by the Chinese authorities understandably adopts very different tones, presenting it as an ambitious regional economic development programme aimed at creating win-win cooperation, increasing understanding and trust, enhancing communication and friendship among the countries of the region, and finally pursuing common prosperity. There are four core principles of the Initiative:

1. *openness and cooperation*, as the BRI is open in nature and does not exclude any party (unlike other forms of international economic cooperation such as the WTO and G20);
2. *harmony and inclusiveness*: some Chinese officials have explicitly stated that all countries are welcome to participate in the Initiative;
3. *market-driven activities*, i.e. although the proposal is political, its implementation must make commercial sense, i.e. the BRI has nothing to do with international aid or anything similar from the Chinese government for economic development; and finally,
4. *shared benefits* for participating countries.

***

Through the BRI, China aims to achieve a number of objectives – difficult to disentangle – both economic and political, domestic and international.

First, the BRI is an exceptional effort by China to sustain its economic growth by exploring new forms of international cooperation with many countries. During the first three decades of economic openness, China achieved very rapid growth, benefiting from the sensational expansion of exports to developed economies and from foreign direct investment, first inbound and then, since the early years of the 21st century, outbound. With the pace of growth steadily declining over the five years from 2008 until 2013, the country's development model seemed to have reached a bottleneck. However, the BRI allows China to look westward for new opportunities to support its next phase of development. In this sense, it represents the most important national development strategy promoted by China in the 21st century.

With the transition to a growth phase characterised by lower rates of investment and capital accumulation than in the Glorious Thirty Years (1980-2010), China is beginning to see the need to encourage development that is less reliant on expanding export volumes and more on increasing export value. Since the 1980s, the high rate of investment was aimed at building up production capacity and conquering foreign markets (in addition to the domestic market, which was already completely protected from foreign competition by Chinese companies), often at the expense of profit margins. However, the great financial crisis of 2008-2009 China was forced to rethink its growth model.

By the end of the 2010s, China had entered a so-called "new normal" phase, with an expected average growth rate between 4.5% and 6.5% in the near future. The search for different growth engines and the transformation of the economic structure have become very urgent tasks. In order to achieve these goals, at the end of 2013 the Party's Central Committee launched a very ambitious reform promising more progress towards a more efficient and open economy. The latter is precisely one of the key points of the reform, particularly with regard to opening up inland and border areas by developing new transport routes and speeding up infrastructure links between neighbouring countries and regions. The ultimate goal here is facilitating the expansion of Chinese companies abroad.

Among the internal economic objectives, priorities are the need to rebalance the gaps between regions, find an outlet for the enormous production capacity accumulated in previous decades and promote exports. There is a particular focus on the countries bordering China to the south and west, namely South-East Asia (altogether a large market of 600 million people) and Central Asia (the area of the world destined to become the next pool of emerging countries). As stated by Vice Chairman of the China International Trade Promotion Council Wang Jinzhen, one goal of the SREB is to promote the development of China's most backward western provinces, such as Gansu, Guangxi, Ningxia, Shanxi, Yunnan and Xinjiang. China hopes that cooperation and development in Central Asia will create a more favourable environment for regional and international security in its western areas, which face the challenges of religious extremism, separatism and terrorism.

In this sense, the BRI creates opportunities to build transport networks that on the one hand open up new markets for the country, allowing it to absorb excess production capacities, and on the other hand foster the development of areas along its western borders. In March 2015, Chinese President Xi Jinping declared that annual trade with countries along the BRI would double within ten years and exceed $2.5 trillion by 2025. In this regard, it is no coincidence that Kazakhstan was the country where President Xi first announced the idea of a New Silk Road: Central Asia is set to become the next emerging area of the world, with a young population on average and rapidly growing demand. Moreover, while the main destination of the maritime part of the BRI is Europe, via the Suez Canal and the Mediterranean, its branches in various East African countries, including Djibouti, Kenya, Madagascar, Mozambique and Tanzania, are intended to support and facilitate the growth of the already-booming trade between Asia and Africa.

***

From China's perspective, the BRI represents a development driver, as it aims not only to build a trade and infrastructure network, but also to integrate the development strategies of participating countries in order to generate synergies and reduce institutional barriers that limit trade and direct investment. This is true for developing countries in Asia, which have vast market potential but whose economic take-off is limited by poor infrastructure, but also for developed economies such as Europe. Here the growth of bilateral trade, investment and other economic exchanges with China has been enormous in recent decades, but the potential of trade and investment relations with China has not been fully exploited, mainly due to restrictions, prohibitions and other institutional barriers.

The BRI's stated interest in enhancing trade relations with large parts of Asia and Africa is closely linked to another objective of the Initiative: reducing China's dependence on seaborne imports of energy commodities.

China's spectacular economic growth over the past three decades has been accompanied by a sharp upsurge in its demand for energy. While its economy continues to grow, albeit at lower rates than before, its dependence on oil and gas imports is set to amplify over the next two decades. China is a major importer of energy resources and supplies oil and gas via transport routes that cross waters controlled by US fleets, such as the Strait of Malacca (more than three-quarters of oil imports and less than one-fifth of oil imports).

That is why energy occupies a prominent place in the BRI, and energy cooperation is one of the main objectives of the SREB. Already in 2013, PetroChina had more than thirty projects abroad along the SREB, including the Aktobe, PK, Mangistaumunaigas and Sino-Kazakhstan oil pipelines in Kazakhstan, the "Amu Darya Right Bank" natural gas project in Turkmenistan, the Ahdab, Rumaila and Halfaya projects in Iraq, and the Central Asia pipeline between Turkmenistan, Uzbekistan and China. According to World Bank estimates, BRI projects in all sectors (already executed, under implementation, and planned) are worth $575 billion, and the total investment in energy accounts for over 45% of the BRI total.

China is currently the world's largest importer of crude oil and its import dependency in this sector is over 70%, above the Chinese government's target cap of around 62%. It is likely that China will continue to be a voracious consumer and importer of oil over the next decade if it wants to reduce its reliance on coal to become carbon neutral by 2060, as announced in October 2020. However, the pace of crude oil imports looks set to slow from previous years, due to a downshift in economic growth, a reduction in energy intensity from heavy industry, the introduction of stricter national environmental laws and, finally, plans to build six to eight nuclear power plants a year until 2030 to cover 10% of electricity consumption.

Meanwhile, China also imports almost half of the natural gas it uses (via pipelines or liquefied natural gas, LNG), mostly from Russia, Central Asia and Australia. Looking ahead, imports of this resource will expand at a rapid pace within a decade, as domestic gas use spreads alongside Beijing's policies to switch from coal to gas, as part of a broader push towards cleaner energy sources. In this regard, it must be said that if any gas supplies were at risk, Beijing could increase its dependence on Russia or use coal temporarily.

This is also why Beijing's primary focus on energy security is oil imports. Importantly, despite efforts to diversify supply sources, China's dependence on Middle Eastern and African supplies still accounts for about two-thirds of its total crude oil imports. This rising reliance on seaborne oil imports at a time of geopolitical tension with the United States and growing instability in the Middle East and North Africa (MENA) is – rightly – causing concern among policymakers in Beijing. The stakes in the MENA region are very high, given the strategic importance of the area in terms of energy supply, along with the extensive economic ties and concern for the welfare and security of the hundreds of Chinese living and working there.

Rising oil prices and tensions in the region can be economically costly for Beijing. More precisely, the annual cost of China's oil imports exceeded $239 billion in 2018, far more than the $75 billion of the previous year, and almost double the 2016 figure. These costs have risen again in 2019, a year in which China imported a record 506 million tonnes of crude oil (which equates to 10.12 million barrels per day), 9.5% above the 2018 level, according to data from China's General Administration of Customs. In short, any significant rise in global oil prices will put pressure on the Chinese economy.

China has some short-term options to alleviate its strategic vulnerabilities associated with increased seaborne supplies and growing instability in several BRI countries. Beijing will rely primarily on diplomatic and economic means to protect these interests in less stable areas. In the medium to long term, if China continues to develop its military capabilities, then persistence in actively securing energy resources, expanding BRI interests, and building strategic alliances may create a need for some level of state and military protection. In the coming decades, therefore, Beijing may become more adventurous in its use of armed forces to advance and protect these interests.

Indeed, according to the March 2015 White Paper of the National People's Congress, the ultimate goal of the project is the establishment of "a stable strategic space conducive to the long-term development of the Chinese economy." Due to the proliferation of Chinese investments in the world, this stability is closely linked to that of the BRI partners and regions covered by the Initiative. The Chinese military is therefore called upon to expand its sphere of action in order to deal with the growing number of threats surrounding Chinese interests abroad. These include, for example, the phenomena of violent opposition to infrastructure and personnel related to BRI projects, as in the case of Vietnam in June 2018 and Pakistan in August 2018. Moreover, within the Sino-Pakistan Economic Corridor (one of the BRI's flagship projects), a special economic zone has been established for the joint production of fighter aircraft, navigation systems and military hardware. The aim here is facilitating the exchange of military technology between China and Pakistan, with potentially serious consequences for regional stability.

The five pillars of the BRI

The central role played by infrastructure in international cooperation and development is the most important feature that distinguishes the BRI from many other international cooperation mechanisms. It is imperative to emphasise this because substantial investment in infrastructure facilitated rapid economic growth during China's reform period and is one of the main drivers of the "Chinese miracle." By contrast, most BRI countries have invested very little in infrastructure, for reasons that vary from country to country – in some cases due to limited financial support, in others simply a lack of planning, construction and coordination capacity. In this sense, the BRI fills a major gap in current international economic governance, i.e. helping to build transnational infrastructure projects, particularly in developing countries.

In early 2014, the IMF called for greater investment in infrastructure around the world as part of efforts to stabilise economic growth, but the lack of funds to support it remains. The Asian Development Bank (ADB) estimates that Asia's infrastructure needs amount to $730 billion a year for at least a decade. However, the ADB is only able to provide $10 billion per year. The newly-established AIIB could help narrow this gap, hopefully by mobilising more resources for infrastructure development from both public and private institutions. There are already a large number of projects under consideration or in the planning stage, mainly in three areas: cross-border high-speed railways, cross-border oil/gas pipelines, and cross-border telecommunications and electricity links.

But the BRI is not just about physical infrastructure. Intangible infrastructure is also part of the story: free trade agreements, project aid agreements and bilateral investment treaties will facilitate infrastructure development.

It seems clear that Chinese leaders want to take the BRI beyond the traditional conception of physical and virtual infrastructure. Speaking about the new MSR at a meeting of several Asian nations prior to the APEC Economic Summit in Beijing in November 2014, Chinese President Xi said that "connecting Asian countries requires a combination of infrastructure, institutions and people-to-people exchanges in five areas: in political communication, infrastructure connectivity, trade links, capital flows and people-to-people understanding."

***

These are the five priority areas of cooperation, according to official Chinese documents: first of all, *political dialogue*. The Initiative aims to create a multi-level intergovernmental mechanism to dialogue on economic and political issues, deepen common interest, reach a new consensus and promote trust between the parties. The aim is to provide political support for cooperation in major projects by appropriately sharing development strategies, action plans and concrete measures.

***

A second important area of cooperation concerns *infrastructure connectivity*. According to the BRI White Paper, the Initiative aims to strengthen plans for the development of basic infrastructure, achieve convergence of technical standards and gradually form an infrastructure network to connect regions in Asia, Europe and Africa. These plans should also promote the low-carbon and green economy, taking full account of the effects of climate change. In fact, the data show that only a fraction of BRI investments have translated into the construction of transport networks: 24% of the total, or 301 projects worth $179.9 billion and including both road and rail transport.

A large part of connectivity relates to energy transport networks. Out of a total of 1247 BRI projects worldwide, 32% (401) are in the energy sector and aim to amplify China's interconnection with the networks of major resource providers, as well as to acquire technological expertise to manage its networks more efficiently. In this context, for example, State Grid Europe Limited (SGEL), a company in the State Grid Corporation of China group, acquired a 35% stake in Italy's CDP Reti, the company that controls Snam, Italgas and Terna, the electricity and gas distribution networks, in 2014. Also, in Southern Europe, the Chinese company acquired 24% of ADMIE, a Greek power company, with an investment of €350 million, in 2016. In July 2018, instead, a similar move against German distributor 50Hertz was prevented through the acquisition of 20% of the company by German state-owned bank KfW. In Africa since 2013, 59 energy, water and mineral extraction-related projects (worth $21.53 billion) have been implemented, with significant investments in the construction of hydropower generation and oil facilities, in addition to coal mining.

To complete the picture of the sector breakdown of BRI projects, it is necessary to mention one that is receiving particular attention: telecommunications. Although still relatively marginal (3% of total projects), this sector is playing an increasingly important role. During 2018, the Pak-China Optical Fibre Cable was completed, a 2950 km long fibre optic network between China and Pakistan, which will significantly speed up the exchange of data and information between the two countries. China's interest in building telecommunications infrastructure was already clear in Africa, where 70% of 4G networks were built by Chinese giant Huawei. Investments in telecommunications within the overall BRI project seem destined to multiply, also in view of China's technological leadership in 5G, where Huawei and ZTE currently have the cheapest solutions at international level (thanks to generous public subsidies and a domestic market protected from foreign competition). But the highly strategic nature of the sector has drawn political attention, with calls for greater caution in opening up to cooperation with Chinese companies.

***

A third objective of the BRI is to promote the expansion of *international trade*. According to the White Paper, the Initiative aims to facilitate interactions, remove barriers, including restrictions on investment, and create a free trade zone between partner countries. The Chinese intention is for the BRI to promote greater economic integration between the areas concerned, thereby facilitating the formation of supra-regional value chains. According to the report on the industrialisation of BRI countries published by the Chinese Academy of Social Sciences, the BRI covers more than 65 countries, which account for more than two-thirds of the world's population, one-third of global GDP, 75% of the world's known energy reserves and about a quarter of world merchandise trade. Currently, 60% of China's trade (by value, and a much higher share by volume) travels by sea, due to the lower transport costs associated with international sea shipments compared to rail transport and the extremely inadequate land transport infrastructure throughout Central Asia.

In this regard, there is no doubt that the BRI aims to stimulate economic development over vast areas of territory stretching from the less developed inland and western provinces of China to the so-called "stan" countries (the appellation derives from the Sanskrit-derived suffix to their names meaning "place, land, nation"), the developing countries of Central Asia and the rest of Asia, as well as the Middle East and East Africa. All Central Asian countries, with the exception of Pakistan, are landlocked, a major disadvantage since access to the sea and the existence of a direct maritime link play a decisive role in determining the cost of trade. In particular, the absence of a direct maritime outlet is estimated to have the same impact on freight rates as an increase in the distance between two countries of 2612 km. By facilitating landlocked countries' access to the sea, the BRI potentially improves their connectivity, thereby promoting their socio-economic development. Chinese investments in the BRI have indeed brought major benefits in terms of increasing the connectivity of recipient countries, in particular maritime connectivity, as measured by a country's integration (whether or not it has direct access to the sea) into the existing network of maritime transport routes (over 90% of world trade is seaborne). Many of the countries concerned suffer from poor connectivity, one of the main obstacles to their development: poor connectivity increases the cost of imported goods and makes exported goods less competitive. In Tajikistan, for example, the incidence of transport costs on the value of an imported container is currently the highest in the world: $10,000 compared to a world average of $1,877. All countries with a large number of BRI projects experienced significant upgrades in their connectivity between 2013 and 2018: these include, for example, Iran (99%), Indonesia (74%), Sri Lanka (68%), Vietnam (59%) and Qatar (11%).

However, there is no consistent pattern of exports to China among the countries with the most BRI projects to date. Of the countries with at least 15 BRI projects, only a few – Myanmar, Sri Lanka, Cambodia, Serbia, Laos and Vietnam – have actually recorded a significant escalation in exports to China (up to almost 300%). In contrast, other countries targeted by many BRI projects, such as Indonesia, have not seen any rise in exports to China, and some have even recorded large reductions, such as Pakistan, Kazakhstan and Saudi Arabia. In the latter, there is a significant gap between the actual results and the prevailing domestic narrative about the benefits of the BRI as a channel to expand access to the Chinese market, which clearly is not due to purely infrastructural issues.

Instead, imports from China have risen significantly and proportionally to the number of BRI projects in the countries considered. The correlation between BRI projects and imports from China is high and positive, i.e. so far, the benefits in terms of market access have generally been greater for China than for the other countries that have joined the Initiative. In this regard, it is worth remembering that the trade objectives set by China with its partner countries are always formulated in terms of "trade" (i.e. the sum of exports and imports) and not in terms of balanced trade relations, which would also require consideration of reciprocity, regulation of uncompetitive practices and copyright infringement.

***

A fourth aim of the BRI is *cultural and scientific cooperation*. According to the White Paper, "the friendly and cooperative spirit is part of the Silk Road culture and should be the basis for the success of the new Initiative." Therefore, the intent is to create certain forms and mechanisms for cultural, academic and talent exchange, training, media cooperation and dialogue among youth and women. The White Paper also mentions international tourism, disease control, joint research centres for laboratories and political parties and parliamentary exchanges as important means of improving mutual understanding and trust.

According to China's Ministry of Education, some 545,000 Chinese students left the country in 2016 to pursue advanced studies abroad, an increase of 36.2% from 2012. The number of students returning to China after completing the course also reached 433,000 in 2016, an increase of 58.6% compared to 2012. Against this backdrop, foreign students from BRI countries are also vying to enrol in Chinese universities: 443,000 international students went on to study in China, up 35.1% from 2012. Hindered by limited university places in their home countries and lured by Chinese scholarships, students from nations along the route of Beijing's infrastructure plan are flocking to China. Chinese universities have become "magnet institutions" for BRI developing countries, making China the world's most outbound student country and at the same time the most popular destination in Asia. China has established educational partnerships with 188 countries and regions, and carried out educational cooperation and exchanges with 46 major international organisations. Agreements on mutual recognition of academic qualifications have been signed with 47 countries and regions.

In addition, there are 512 Confucius Institutes and 1074 Confucius Classrooms scattered in 140 countries and regions around the world; among them, 135 institutes and 129 classrooms are located in 51 countries along the BRI. Over 67 countries have also established policies to include Chinese language teaching in their national education systems. Chinese language courses and programmes are offered in over 170 countries. The number of people learning and using the Chinese language worldwide has reached 100 million.

In 2015, China launched the Silk Road University Alliance, which brings together more than 130 universities from five continents and is coordinated by China's Jiaotong University in Xi'an. This alliance aims to develop cooperation between its members and to promote the BRI initiative in higher education. Another example is HKUST Business School in Hong Kong which has joined forces with Moscow School of Management SKOLKOVO to launch a new Executive MBA programme for Eurasia.

The Chinese Academy of Sciences (CAS) has provided more than 1.8 billion renminbi (approximately $268 million) since 2013 to build science and technology projects in association with the BRI initiative. The Alliance of International Science Organisations (ANSO) was launched in November 2016 under the BRI and is composed of scientific research organisations from BRI participating countries and international organisations. According to SAC President Chunli Bai, ANSO members have recently clarified its vision and mission, pledging to make it an international organisation with great influence in promoting, organising and implementing scientific innovation.

Also falling within the sphere of cultural cooperation is the set of agreements between Chinese and foreign news agencies. Notably, in April 2019, China silently launched a new media group: the Belt and Road News Network (BRNN), whose mission is to promote "understanding, friendship and cooperation, and form a collaborative mechanism" (Albert, 2019) among countries and regions participating in the Initiative. The BRNN was first suggested by Chinese President Xi at the first *Belt and Road Forum* in 2017. The platform is based in Beijing and is chaired by the *People's Daily*, China's largest newspaper group and the official source of the Chinese Communist Party Central Committee. According to the network's charter, the BRNN board consists of 14 members from China and 26 others from Asia, Africa, Europe, Latin America, the Middle East and Eurasia (Bangladesh, Belarus, Egypt, Ethiopia, France, Indonesia, Kazakhstan, Laos, Mexico, Mongolia, Myanmar, the Netherlands, Nigeria, Pakistan, Portugal, Russia, South Africa, South Korea, Spain, Sudan, Tanzania, the U.A.E., the United Kingdom and Zambia). BRNN activities include study tours, seminars, awards, access to news archives and databases, workshops and training programmes. Separately, *People's Daily* describes the BRNN website as a hub for communication, uploading, downloading, and sharing content among network members. The network claims to provide content in six languages: Chinese, Arabic, English, French, Russian and Spanish, but it is still only *People's Daily* that manages the websites in all those languages. The architecture of the site also suggests that BRNN will seek to provide comprehensive data and information on BRI projects and investments. Therefore, in all likelihood it will be increasingly difficult to distinguish between reported data and Chinese political propaganda on the benefits of BRI.

***

Finally, among the fundamental pillars of the BRI are *financial cooperation and support*. According to PBoC Governor Yi Gang, with respect to the future of financial connectivity, the subject of the second *Belt and Road Forum* held in Beijing on 25 April 2019, China has made great progress in terms of the financial support given to the BRI.

First, China's financial institutions have provided the equivalent of more than $440 billion for the BRI, including more than 320 billion renminbi funnelled through channels dedicated to the foreign circulation of the renminbi. China's capital market provided more than 500 billion renminbi in equity financing for relevant enterprises. In addition, BRI countries and corporations raised more than 65 billion renminbi by issuing *panda bonds* in the Chinese market, which are renminbi-denominated bonds issued by parties based outside the PRC (we will return to this instrument in more detail in Chapter 3).

Second, financial services have become more sophisticated. By the end of 2018, eleven Chinese banks had opened 76 branches in 28 countries along the BRI, and about fifty banks in 22 BRI countries have business operations in China. They provide a wider variety of financial products and services, including credit, guarantees, bond underwriting, mergers and acquisitions, risk management, clearing and so on.

Third, international cooperation has deepened. The PBoC has signed bilateral local currency swap agreements with twenty-one central banks along the BRI. Interbank cooperation mechanisms in the BRI have been working steadily to improve dialogue among financial institutions, including the China-CEEC (Central and Eastern European Countries) Interbank Association and the SCO (Shanghai Cooperation Organization) Interbank Association. The PBoC Governor also stated that opening up China's financial sector can play a role in supporting and promoting the BRI, as the development and accessibility of the local currency bond market effectively mobilises long-term capital. Increased use of local currency also helps to reduce exchange rate and currency mismatch risks. In short, not only does financial connectivity support the smooth and sustainable development of the BRI, but the BRI itself requires an open, market-based investment and financing system, which China claims to want to achieve.

BRI: China's foreign policy shift

Originally aimed at connecting China to Western European markets by land and sea, the BRI has now expanded to Africa and Latin America, and its objectives go far beyond transport networks. The BRI is seeking to upgrade China's international connectivity and integration, not only in terms of infrastructure, logistics and trade, but also culturally, energetically and financially, and has become a foreign policy tool in its own right.

However, in the past, under the influence of Deng Xiaoping's suggestion to "hide one's capabilities, bide one's time, get things done where possible," Chinese leaders seemed to have a "small country" mentality. The leadership change in 2012 marked a major shift in the strategic thinking of Chinese leaders from a "small country" to a "big country" mindset. Since then, the new leadership has realised that the country has no choice but to coordinate with its major partners when the international consequences of China's rise are at stake, or risk policies of containment, as was the case with the Trump administration's US policy towards Beijing. With this change of mindset, Chinese policymakers have begun to focus on both international and domestic markets and to plan domestic reforms in light of their global consequences. In this sense, the Third Plenum of the 18th Party Congress called for "adapting to the new situation of globalisation."

During the first decades of economic reforms, Chinese leaders mostly followed the principles laid down by Deng Xiaoping, namely "keeping a low profile in the management of international affairs," but respecting this instruction is becoming more and more difficult. China is already the world's second largest economy and contributes one third of the world's GDP growth. Its global influence is most evident in international markets for labour-intensive manufactured goods and raw materials. In 2015, Chinese influence took a further step forward, when the Fed recognised China's slowing growth as an important factor in its own monetary policy decisions, while shockwaves rippled around the world, triggered by the volatility of the renminbi exchange rate and the volatility of the A-share market (securities of Chinese companies available to local Chinese investors and foreign traders who have been granted Qualified Foreign Institutional Investors (QFII) status by the Beijing government).

***

The BRI is the most ambitious Chinese international policy initiative in history. Rarely had China played an active economic role beyond its borders. To date, according to official Chinese sources, the number of countries that have joined the BRI by signing a Memorandum of Understanding with China is 138. For some countries listed as signatories to a BRI MoU, independent information that is available is contradictory. Austria, Benin, Comoros, Democratic Republic of Congo, Dominica (an island in the Lesser Antilles), Niger and the Russian Federation, for example, have not publicly confirmed or denied signing a full MoU. The BRI countries are spread across all continents: 38 are in Sub-Saharan Africa; 34 in Europe and Central Asia (including 18 European Union countries); 25 in East Asia and the Pacific; 17 in the Middle East and North Africa; 18 in Latin America and the Caribbean; and 6 in South-East Asia.

***

With the MoU signed in Rome in March 2019, Italy has also joined China's roster of partners in the BRI project. Our country is potentially a strategic terminal hub in the BRI, one of the most important among the 65 countries involved. First of all, together with Holland and Poland, it is one of the main entry points for Chinese goods into Europe. Italy's geostrategic advantage as a gateway to continental Europe has increased since the substantial Chinese investment in the Greek port of Piraeus (two thirds of which was acquired by the Chinese COSCO), which has now become the main hub for Chinese trade in Europe. From Piraeus, Chinese containers continue on their way to the richer European markets. This is why China has begun to look to the Upper Adriatic as a strategic outlet: to connect maritime trade in the Mediterranean with Austria, Germany, Switzerland, Slovenia and Hungary. The Adriatic Sea certainly has an advantage over the Tyrrhenian Sea, the orographic conformation and the infrastructural difficulties of its coastline (with the presence, in particular, of numerous railway and road tunnels) do not facilitate the development of further logistical lines inland.

Intense cooperation has long existed between Beijing and the Adriatic side of the peninsula. Trieste, for example, is part of the Trihub project, a component of the framework agreement between the EU and China aimed at promoting reciprocal infrastructure investments. China Merchants Group could make new investments in the port of Trieste, while the giant CCCC intends to make a large financial commitment (of around $1.3 billion) to the construction of a deep-water quay in the port of Venice. Also, in the Adriatic, in 2018 China Merchant Group invested €10 million in the port of Ravenna with the aim of making the city the European hub for marine engineering and oil & gas.

On the other side of our peninsula, despite the constraints posed by the orographic conformation, China has also been interested in the Ligurian logistics landscape, which represents a potential hub to reach the markets of France and the Iberian Peninsula. In this regard, since 2016 Beijing has secured a direct presence through a 49.9% stake in the Vado Ligure container terminal (40% through COSCO Shipping and 9.9% held by the Port of Qingdao). This port facility will be equipped with the most advanced technologies in terms of automation and will be able to accommodate large ships.

***

The BRI is part of China's strategy to augment Beijing's influence and weight in the world, economically, politically and militarily. Although it is officially presented as an infrastructure project for economic development through greater regional and international integration of the country, the BRI has an established link with the People's Liberation Army (PLA) and its naval branch (PLA Navy). Through BRI projects, China is equipping itself with the ability to extend its geo-strategic reach beyond regional borders. For example, the construction in April 2016 of the first overseas naval base in Doraleh, an extension of Djibouti port, provides China with access to maritime routes distant from Chinese territory, which has allowed the PLA Navy to establish a presence in the Red Sea, which means also moving closer to the Mediterranean Sea. The solid logistics provided by the BRI also allow China to support its military power from a distance.

This is why the BRI is of concern to the US and the major advanced economies. In the current global geopolitical scenario, with increasing challenges to globalisation and multilateralism – the foundation of the liberal international order born out of World War II – the world is once again at a historic turning point. During Trump's presidency, economic and political developments in the United States, with the withdrawal from the Trans-Pacific Partnership (TPP) and his protectionist trade policies and immigration restrictions, have cast doubt on the future of US participation in global governance. On the contrary, China has taken a clear stance to defend globalisation and promote a new multilateralism, confirmed by President Xi's speech in Davos on 17 January 2017 and on 25 January 2021. Not surprisingly, tensions have been mounting between China and the great powers. The first type of tension concerns a possible conflict between existing and rising powers. China is expected to overtake the United States in terms of aggregate GDP, to become the world's largest economy in less than a decade, and it has been positioning itself as a leader of the developing and emerging world. However, China is still a developing country itself, with neither the capacity nor the obligation to defend and lead globalisation on its own.

***

As it aims to improve connectivity between a number of previously separate regions (Europe, the post-Soviet space, Central, East and South Asia, the Middle East), the BRI is in fact a comprehensive long-term strategy to build an area in which China serves as the economic and geopolitical centre of gravity. Thus, in addition to Central Asia, both Russia and Ukraine clearly have crucial positions in the Initiative, explicitly envisaged by the Chinese leadership. More specifically, the SREB is a response to the integration process that is already underway within Eurasia and which, long debated by Russia and some of the largest Central Asian republics, led to the creation of the Eurasian Economic Union (EEU) in 2015. The BRI aims to act as a binder for regional cooperation and integration projects already underway, with the broader goal of connecting East Asia to Europe via Central Asia. In this context, Ukraine is very important because of its geographical location between Russia and Europe, which also explains why China has recently intensified cooperation there in the development of the SREB.

Although most of the public debate and attention has been devoted to the implications of the BRI in Central Asia, no less crucial for the overall success of the initiative is the MENA region. It is indeed a truly strategic place where the "Belt" joins the "Road," where the two main land and sea routes meet, as the China-Central Asia-West Asia economic corridor reaches Iran and Turkey and the Mediterranean Sea, the Red Sea and the

Suez Canal. This is also the reason behind the decision of many Middle Eastern countries to join the AIIB, the main financing institution of the BRI. Of these, Oman and Turkey are likely to be the countries most affected by the BRI corridors.

Europe, the arrival point of the BRI both by land and sea, is the final geographical destination and the most important political partner. The Initiative aims to ease economic and political relations between two major economic powers, at a time when geopolitical tensions in various parts of Asia and with the United States pose a serious risk to the future of multilateral cooperation. Even before the birth of the BRI, the EU and China had already held regular dialogues on rail, maritime, air, customs facilitation, as well as other connectivity issues, through the *EU-China 2020 Strategic Agenda for Cooperation* signed in 2013.

However, not all European countries are equally essential to the BRI. Indeed, within Europe, BRI projects are concentrated in two particular regions: Central and Eastern Europe and the European Mediterranean countries. Meanwhile, in September 2015, the European Commission and the Chinese government signed a *Memorandum on the EU-China Connectivity Platform* to strengthen synergies between China's BRI and EU connectivity initiatives such as the Trans-European Transport Network TEN-T.

Last but not least, the BRI is likely to have profound and lasting implications for economic and political relations around the world, representing a real turning point in international trade relations, if it does in fact shift at least some of the main international trade routes from sea today in favour of land tomorrow. The modification of the international trade route network may have profound implications for the geopolitical relationship between China and Europe, Central Asia and Russia, and also within the entire Pacific region. In fact, the main corridors of current trade in goods, mineral oils and gas by sea are likely to migrate westwards, from the South China Sea to Middle Eastern routes.

Why financial cooperation is essential in the BRI

An important part of the realisation of the BRI is financial integration among the countries involved. There are at least three reasons for this: first, although the BRI is an initiative of the Chinese government, it involves many countries, now over a hundred, and requires huge financial resources. So it is unthinkable that its financing should be limited to Chinese capital. Moreover, since the renminbi is not an international currency, although it circulates to some extent outside China, this implies that BRI projects have to be financed with resources denominated mainly in foreign currencies (in particular dollars). This creates a "dollar dependency" that reduces the possibility of projects being financed from China. From this perspective, the internationalisation of the renminbi facilitates the completion of the BRI, contributing to the realisation of the five types of connectivity.

There are three main channels through which greater international circulation of the renminbi would facilitate the realisation of BRI.

First, the internationalisation of the renminbi would provide financial support to complete the BRI, which consists of many projects, with infrastructure construction being the largest cost item. These projects are potentially conducive to the economic development of beneficiary countries, insofar as connectivity is a precondition for development, but they require huge investments and a long construction period. Moreover, they do not necessarily manifest an apparent direct effect, as their indirect effect is strong but difficult to measure. Therefore, they are considered as public goods, i.e. they have many positive externalities. For example, it is unlikely that the operation of a high-speed railway would generate profits simply from toll revenues. However, the construction of a high-speed railway will have a number of domino effects: it motivates the mobilisation of labour and technology from the countries it reaches; it can stimulate economic and commercial communication; it can improve regional scientific and technological standards; it can increase the volume of trade and it can promote service industries, including tourism.

Second, increased international circulation of the renminbi provides sufficient liquidity to finance trade, and trade between China and countries along the BRI is growing rapidly. According to data from the Chinese Customs Service, trade turnover with the five Central Asian countries exceeded $41.7 billion in 2018. While Central Asia accounts for 0.8% of Chinese imports and 0.9% of Chinese exports, the region's dependence on China is rising. China is now the destination of about 22% of all Central Asian exports and the source of 37% of their imports. Central Asian countries have asymmetrical trade relations with China. China is also the largest buyer of gas and resources from Central Asian countries. At the same time, it is the largest investor for Uzbekistan and the second largest investor for Kyrgyzstan. With the gradual development of the BRI, regional trade should continue to grow, which will generate greater demand for trade finance and liquidity. In this sense, the internationalisation of the renminbi promotes the development of the BRI by providing adequate liquidity. On the one hand, countries along the BRI may have access to renminbi trade finance, but they can also accumulate renminbi assets; on the other hand, China has signed currency swap agreements with several countries, which allow the counterparties to provide renminbi loans to domestic enterprises to pay for goods imported from China.

The third aspect to consider is that the internationalisation of the renminbi reduces the exchange rate risk of using a third currency, i.e. the dollar. The choice of international settlement currency is determined by fluctuations in currency supply, exchange rate variations, transaction costs and interest rates. Of these, the most important factor is transaction costs. Currently, the US dollar is the dominant international settlement currency, for three reasons: first, most commodities are priced in dollars so the use of the dollar in the settlement of international trade can reduce transaction costs. Second, the dollar is also an official reserve currency for most countries. Third, the exchange rate and value of the US dollar are relatively stable. For all these reasons, the dollar is the most widely used currency in international trade transactions, even though the share of US trade in the world total has been declining over time. However, after the great financial crisis of 2008-2009, the volatility of the dollar increased dramatically, especially when the launch of quantitative easing exacerbated its devaluation. Thus, both parties in an international trade contract face greater volatility when using the dollar for transactions. Since China is a major trading partner for countries along the BRI, using the renminbi as a settlement currency in regional trade could actually reduce the risks of using a third currency. In recent times, the use of the renminbi as a payment and invoicing currency has led to increasing benefits, so that it has become much more widely accepted globally.

A final, particularly important and topical aspect concerns international e-commerce between China and a growing number of trading partners. As this number is rapidly multiplying, especially along the BRI, improved financial cooperation would immensely benefit cross-border trade in goods, and in particular greater internationalisation of the renminbi would intensely accelerate e-commerce. Indeed, China's increased cross-border e-commerce promotes the international pricing function of its currency: until 2004, the share of prices expressed in domestic currency was much lower than that in currencies of developed countries but in more recent years it has augmented, because Chinese consumers are the world's largest e-commerce marketplace, and foreign e-commerce firms are more and more willing to price their products in renminbi to benefit Chinese customers. As cross-border e-commerce with renminbi pricing grows, so does the need for the renminbi to also become a recognised and accepted international settlement currency.

***

This brings us to the issue of the internationalisation of the renminbi, which is still a non-convertible currency, i.e. one that does not circulate freely outside Chinese borders. Said internationalisation has been a goal of the Beijing government since at least 2009. To date, the impact of this strategy is measured not so much by the still-limited scope of China's currency and financial sector reforms, but simply by the strong growth in the use of the renminbi currency for payments in China's international trade: currently around 25% of these transactions, up from less than 1% in 2009. The renminbi is sixth in the ranking of the most widely used currencies in international payments, according to data regularly published by SWIFT, with a share of 1.6%. This is an extremely modest share, compared with that of the dollar (40.6%) and the euro (33.3%). However, fairly liquid and diversified markets for the renminbi now exist in Hong Kong, London, Singapore and most international financial centres around the world.

Despite this progress, the renminbi is clearly still a currency in the making and not a truly international one. It is by no means a "big currency" like the dollar, whose use extends beyond the realm of international transactions. It is true, to paraphrase Nobel Prize winner Robert Mundell, that "great nations have great currencies," the lack of a real currency – and thus the need to use the dollar in most international transactions – limits China's ability to use its considerable financial resources to achieve its economic and political goals. If the renminbi were an internationally circulating currency, this would reduce China's dependence on the dollar. The fact that the renminbi is exclusively a domestic currency represents a major obstacle to China's economic and political objectives, weakening the country in both bilateral and multilateral international relations. This is why the BRI also includes the pillar of financial cooperation, in synergy with the other objectives of the Initiative.

***

China has long pursued the goal of greater financial integration with the rest of the world, albeit more cautiously than other emerging economies. In fact, China's large balance of payments surpluses, both on the current account and the financial account, have put upward pressure on its currency, something that Beijing is neither prepared nor willing to accept. The monetary authorities have therefore partly allowed greater exchange rate flexibility, but at the same time have actively intervened in the currency market to prevent an appreciation of the currency, thus accumulating huge amounts of reserves: between 1990 and 2010, reserves increased from almost $29 billion (8.3% of GDP) to over $2.8 trillion (almost 50% of GDP). Since then, they have risen to a peak of $4 trillion in early 2015 before stabilising between $3 trillion and $3,200 billion as of 2016. In August 2020 it was $3,165 billion.

In order to better understand the situation in which China finds itself today from a currency point of view, we need to open a parenthesis on a monetary policy choice problem based on the traditional Mundell-Fleming paradigm developed in the 1960s. This is a trilemma of international monetary economics known as the "impossible trinity." It states that countries necessarily face a trilemma regarding these three objectives: free movement of capital, stable exchange rate management and monetary autonomy. The problem is, no country can control all three simultaneously. Although China has never completely abolished all capital controls, there have always been various ways to channel money into the country and to get it out as well. At the same time, the renminbi started to fluctuate more against the dollar, but China was also able to raise or lower interest rates without impacting the exchange rate too much. This is why the Chinese authorities have often argued that China has actually managed to circumvent the logic of the irreconcilable trio by negotiating on each of the three objectives.

As China has chosen to open its capital account very slowly, and continues to actively intervene in the foreign exchange market to stabilise its currency, it faces the fundamental challenge of maintaining the autonomy of its domestic monetary policy and thus price stability. Already in its recovery from the Great Recession of 2008-2009, it had to contend with a serious credit boom that fuelled inflationary concerns. China's monetary authorities curbed the problem by raising banks' reserve requirement ratios, but within the trilemma the goal of monetary policy independence was seriously jeopardised.

In this respect, the experience of emerging markets suggests that the trilemma ignores the possibility that, through an increase in international reserves, countries could pursue limited but gradual financial integration without giving up rate stability and monetary independence. This was certainly the case for China, which chose a singular path, i.e. it clearly prioritised minimising exchange rate fluctuations as a macroeconomic management tool. The objective of exchange rate stabilisation was given greater political weight, perhaps at the expense of monetary independence and especially the opening of the capital account. In this way, China has been able to slowly augment financial openness by gradually accumulating foreign exchange reserves.

***

After 1979, the PBoC managed its exchange rate for decades by maintaining controls on capital flows, without giving up an independent monetary policy. However, over the past two decades capital has become substantially more mobile (i.e. harder to control) and China has registered substantial capital inflows, mainly due to huge amounts of foreign direct investments. Most of all, short-term speculative capital movements can easily circumvent capital restrictions. Overall, China has liberalised its capital flows over the years, but the authorities still prefer to exercise control over these flows and their effects on domestic industries. One can expect that future progress on the BRI will put more pressure on China to further liberalise financial markets and require a greater openness to free capital flows. But the Chinese authorities are more reluctant than ever to move towards financial and capital market liberalisation, because this would inevitably result in greater financial instability. And instability, not only political but also economic, is unacceptable to the Chinese government.

At the same time, China's exchange rate is becoming more like a regulated fluctuation than a real fixed exchange rate, since large amounts of capital moving in and out of China have made the renminbi more vulnerable to speculation. For this reason the authorities have gradually relaxed their tight control of the exchange rate. The PBoC has always tried to keep the exchange rate low and stable so as not to lose price competitiveness in foreign markets, as the renminbi has been rather undervalued for many years and continual pressure from financial market forces have pushed toward appreciation. Eventually, the PBoC allowed the currency to partially float to the extent that it does not harm domestic industries. As a result, monetary sovereignty is also somewhat diminished, as the PBoC uses it mainly for maintaining the exchange rate. Today we can assume that the rapid growth of public debt will also require some adjustment of monetary policy, which should become an essential instrument for stabilising the economy and not only the exchange rate.

Over the past two decades, especially in the years leading up to the 2008-2009 financial crisis, the Chinese authorities have repeatedly tried to achieve all the objectives of the trilemma. However, since the onset of the Great Financial Crisis, the focus has once again centered on currency stability combined with increased capital mobility as a response to an appreciation of the renminbi in the years leading up to the crisis. On the other hand, from 2014 onwards, policy changed again in favour of a combination of monetary autonomy with easier capital circulation, to the detriment of exchange rate stability. Since the Mundell-Fleming model underestimates the role of monetary sterilisation policy, which China has adopted on a massive scale, the government has been able to bend or circumvent the trilemma described above and, by doing so, to refute the theory that the trio is completely irreconcilable.

Today, the ultimate goal of the Chinese authorities is also to maintain financial stability. After the global financial crisis, China was confident that it had circumvented the trilemma, with the development of shadow banking (i.e. all the financial instruments perform credit intermediation functions typically carried out by banks, and at the same time reduce the burden of banking regulation or circumvent banking supervision). In light of this, together with the need for greater internationalisation of the renminbi since the late 2000s, according to Aizenman (2011) China finds that challenging the trilemma is at odds with the quest for greater financial stability. The question then arises as to what extent the authorities can circumvent or bend a trilemma. Indeed, China aspires not only to have a fixed (or in fact more managed) exchange rate, an independent monetary policy and the free flow of capital at least to some extent, but is now also trying to preserve financial stability by protecting itself from short-term capital inflows. The tendency of the authorities to defy the trilemma as much as possible will make it more difficult to keep the financial system stable and may lead to even greater market distortions. Moreover, according to some scholars, the PBoC is also breaking its promises to the IMF on renminbi convertibility (as we will see in Chapter 2) by erecting new barriers to renminbi conversion in order to control capital flows. In this sense, instead of circumventing the trilemma, China would for now have sacrificed both capital flows and monetary autonomy to preserve monetary stability. At the moment, it therefore has to manage a particularly complex situation on the currency front, to which the implementation of the BRI could benefit, in the ways we shall see below.

***

The huge amount of resources needed to finance the projects along the BRI could undermine the sustainability of the whole Initiative. It is estimated that the total investment needed to cover transport infrastructure (excluding electricity, water and other infrastructure) is between $1 and $8 trillion. This amount of money has involved many different sources. According to a 2016 PwC study, the entire BRI will be financed by the following sources: 50% national budgets, 20% national development banks, 25% private sector, 3% to 4% multilateral development banks, 1% to 2% South-South flows. Despite resistance from Western countries because of the overlap with IMF purposes, three financial institutions have been used to support this project, namely the Silk Road Fund, the AIIB and the New Development Bank. Particularly important for the BRI is the AIIB, which, as already mentioned, is a multilateral development bank aimed at supporting infrastructure construction, especially in Asian countries. Founded by Chinese President Xi in October 2013, it started operations in January 2016 and has since approved more than thirty projects. Although the official objective of the institution is to finance infrastructure in Asia, it is sometimes seen as a key tool of China's foreign policy as well as development policy. Regardless of its various objectives to date, the BRI and the AIIB are working in significant synergy and the AIIB is expected to serve as one of the most substantial sources of financing for infrastructure investment.

The US dollar recapitalisations of the China Development Bank and the China Export-Import Bank also play a prominent role in BRI projects, so it is clear that funding comes mainly from China's huge financial resources. However, the time has come and gone when China accumulated huge foreign exchange reserves, which had almost reached $4 trillion in June 2014. Now the Chinese economy has slowed down, foreign exchange reserves have shrunk by almost $1 trillion due to massive capital outflows, the shadow banking system has become larger and the balance sheets of regular banks are burdened with many non-performing loans, which continue to be refinanced and do not leave much room for the loans needed to finance the BRI. Chinese banks have so far been the largest lenders and the multilateral development organisations geared towards this goal certainly do not have the financial means to provide this kind of support. Even the AIIB has so far only approved investments of $1.7 billion in 2016, $2.5 billion in 2017 and $3.3 billion in 2018 on BRI projects. The "dollar constraint" has undoubtedly reduced the scope for China to finance BRI projects, at least in hard currency. Against this backdrop, financing options are limited, bringing China back to the trilemma quandary mentioned above.

Despite the inherent limitations of the renminbi and thus of Chinese finance, the United States continues to perceive China as a threat and the renminbi as a potential competitor to the dollar, even though the dollar will continue to be the currency underpinning the international monetary system for many years to come. The reasons for these fears lie in the characteristics of the particular strategy chosen by the Chinese government to manage the transition to greater international circulation of the renminbi. In fact, there have been plans in Beijing for some time to build a true international renminbi circulation area that would provide a currency stability system, an investment and financing system, and an integrated credit information system in Asia, along with other financial initiatives in the pipeline to deepen multilateral financial cooperation, as we will see in Chapter 2.

2020, a turning point?

While China has said that the impact of Covid-19 on the BRI has been minimal, the first quarter of 2020 saw a significant slowdown in new projects, and the uncertain pace of the recovery of the Chinese economy could divert attention from BRI projects in the near future as well. In addition, to provide relief to many economies that are heavily indebted to China on BRI projects, it is plausible that Beijing will work with major lenders and multilateral organisations such as the ADB, IMF and World Bank.

In any case, 2020 is a watershed year for the BRI in many ways: in terms of its characteristics, its significance, and its implications. In terms of characteristics, the BRI is now worth almost $4 trillion, of which $137.43 billion has been announced out of 184 projects approved in the first quarter of 2020 (Refinitiv data). In terms of value, transport accounts for 47% of all BRI projects, or $1,880 billion, followed by energy and water at 23% ($926 billion).

The new ranking of major recipient countries is quite different from past rankings. Overall, at the end of Q1 2020, according to Belt and Road News, Russia retained its place as the largest BRI recipient, with 126 projects for a total value of $296 billion, including both BRI investment projects and those funded directly by China. Russia has used its geographical proximity to China and its natural resources to emerge as an important partner for Beijing. The Power of Siberia Gas Pipeline project is perhaps the best illustration of the potential of the Sino-Russian alliance. Russia's Gazprom is building a 3,000 km natural gas pipeline for this project, which runs through the Irkutsk and Amur regions and the Republic of Sakha (Yakutia) in northeast China. The $55 billion project is among the largest in the BRI (according to Refinitiv). In December 2019, the first phase of Power of Siberia was commissioned and the first deliveries of Russian gas to China through the pipeline began. "This is a truly historic event, not only for the global energy market, but above all for us, for Russia and for China," Russian President Vladimir Putin said at the launch of the project's first phase. "This step takes Russian-Chinese strategic cooperation in the energy sector to a qualitatively new level and brings us closer to [the fulfilment of] the task, set together with Chinese President Xi, of raising bilateral trade to $200 billion by 2024. Once completed, the project will export 38 billion cubic metres of gas to China every year for 30 years, generating an estimated $400 billion for Moscow. The deal will make China the second largest customer of Russian gas after Germany.

Saudi Arabia is second, with $185 billion in 111 projects, and Malaysia is third with 57 projects worth a total of $146 billion. Today, the UK is the fourth largest recipient of BRI investment, with active projects worth $139 billion covering the energy and water, transport and real estate sectors. Interestingly, the UK, which debuted in the top 10 projects in December 2019, has maintained its position as the fourth largest BRI beneficiary by value; the world's sixth largest economy has 13 active projects worth $139 billion in the power and water, transport and real estate sectors. Examples are the partnerships between state-owned companies China General Nuclear Power Corporation (CGN) and EDF in the development of the Hinkley Point C nuclear and power plants (CGN has a 33.5% stake in $29 billion). The UK and China have also been engaged, according to a BBC report, in preliminary discussions to give China Railway Construction Corporation (CRCC), another Chinese state-owned company, a role in the construction of the multi-billion dollar HS2 high-speed rail line.

All this now makes it clear that the BRI is not so much or not only an infrastructure development project (both physical and digital). Instead it also encompasses many other spheres of cooperation, including, in addition to energy, also health and finance for example. In the midst of the pandemic in the spring of 2020, China re-launched the so-called "Health Silk Road" (which had already been in place since 2017). The aim here was to show how the BRI infrastructure network (but especially the bilateral arrangements for its implementation) could serve as a mechanism for the delivery of medical services and humanitarian aid. In addition, it is becoming increasingly clear that the financial Silk Road is a key pillar of the entire BRI (hence the idea of writing this book): a wide range of cross-border financial policy programmes are in place, including a series of currency swap agreements (to compensate for the non-convertibility of the renminbi), the development of an Asian bond market and the foreign issuance of renminbi-denominated bonds.

As for the meaning of the BRI, beyond the ecumenical overtones that often evoke the goal of "forging a community with a common destiny," a more concrete and immediate goal is evident: managing the national overcapacity accumulated by SOEs during the economic boom years (1980-2010). Many companies benefit from generous government subsidies to become global champions in their sectors. The BRI also offers China the opportunity to build its Greater Bay Area (GBA), a conurbation of nine of Guangdong province, namely Guangzhou, Shenzhen, Zhuhai, Foshan, Huizhou, Dongguan, Zhongshan, Jiangmen and Zhaoqing, plus the two special administrative regions of Hong Kong and Macao. The area already has a huge impact on the whole economy: despite being home to just over 71 million people, or only 5% of China's population, it produces 37% of the Asian giant's GDP and 12% of its exports. On its own, the GBA is already the world's fourth largest exporter and the 15th largest economy in the world, larger even than Spain.

As for the implications of the BRI, much has been said about China leveraging its influence on emerging markets and how this could lure them into a "debt trap" that would make them financially vulnerable to Chinese interests. However, according to the Rhodium Group, which examined forty cases of China's external debt rescheduling, a different picture emerges: more than one of the emerging economies that enthusiastically participated in the BRI had been highly leveraged for some time before embarking on the project. Indeed, cases of over-indebtedness to China create a high-risk situation for the creditor side as well, and it is likely that there will be more cases of distress in a few years' time, as many Chinese projects were launched from 2013 to 2016. In fact, since 2013, China has invested $690 billion in BRI projects in 72 countries, with about $280 billion in 44 countries that have no agency rating or are not considered investment grade, according to the International Finance Institute. A report by the Centre for Global Development found that 23% of BRI countries were at high risk of indebtedness even before the pandemic, and today there are at least eight countries at risk of over-indebtedness, including Djibouti, Mongolia, Kyrgyzstan, Laos, Maldives, Pakistan and Montenegro. Pakistan, for example, recently received a $1.4 billion loan from the IMF to address the economic slowdown caused by the Coronavirus epidemic.

Overall, then, the BRI continues to weave its web well beyond transport infrastructure. It is a composite, forward-looking and, above all, very malleable initiative designed to become the format of China's bilateral relations with the rest of the world, especially with developing countries. Indeed, this seems to be the intention of influential academic thinkers in China, including Chinese scholar Yao Yang, dean of the National Development School at Peking University, who proposed in autumn 2020 to transform the BRI into an operational institution for the developing world, with headquarters in Europe. According to Yao, the BRI should be an organisation that provides expertise and advice to developing countries, following the example of the Organisation for Economic Cooperation and Development (OECD), which provides knowledge and advice to developed countries.

2 The Art of Finance, with Chinese Characteristics

China has been the world's largest exporter since 2009, and in 2019 foreign trade accounted for over 35% of its GDP. Every day, China exports an average of almost $8 billion and imports almost $6 billion. Thus, every day China has to manage a huge mass of cash in dollars and convert them into renminbi, as the use of the renminbi as a medium of exchange, unit of account and store of value is deliberately restricted by the Chinese authorities.

China's large trade surplus since the mid-1980s has entailed complex monetary and currency management, as well as strong financial and political dependence on the dollar. The desire to maintain a restricted convertibility of the renminbi and capital controls (to prevent them from fleeing the country in search of better employment opportunities) limit the circulation of the national currency outside China. Thus, the Chinese monetary authorities, who do not want to give up the stability of a protected financial and currency system, find themselves, in a nutshell, having to encourage the use of the renminbi abroad.

Today, the BRI is offering a historic opportunity for the internationalisation of the renminbi: by increasing trade and investment in partner countries, it is significantly boosting demand for the renminbi outside Chinese borders thus creating the conditions for extending its circulation abroad. The most interesting aspect of this strategy is the extremely innovative and ingenious way in which China intends to circulate the renminbi around the world: a system of controlled convertibility based on renminbi deposits in a network of banks scattered throughout various countries. More recently, as mentioned above and as we will see later, circulation is being proliferated through the issuance of a digital currency that can also be used in international payments.

The renminbi's long march

It is not possible to identify a precise date when Beijing first moved towards the goal of internationalising its national currency. Discussions began as early as 2002, but it was not until 2006 that a significant breakthrough came with the publication of *The Timing, Path, and Strategies of RMB Internationalisation* by a study group set up by the PBoC. It concluded that the time had finally come to promote the internationalisation of the renminbi to improve China's international status and competitiveness, as well as its influence and power in the international economy. However, it was not until the global financial crisis of 2008 that there was a marked change in attitude on the part of the Chinese authorities, who had become aware that the country's vast dollar reserves made it vulnerable to a sudden change in exchange rates.

Until the publication of that report, China had had one of the most tightly controlled currencies in the world, protected from all sorts of currency restrictions and controls on international capital flows. But how could China promote the international use of the renminbi if the currency is not and will not be, at least for a little while longer, easily convertible? Past experience with currencies that have gone international, such as the Deutsche mark, yen and euro, shows that in no case has a path been planned by the issuing authorities. Internationalisation was determined solely by market demand-side preferences, which is a precondition for a national currency to be accepted and start circulating outside the issuing country. Therefore, in the absence of a model for the creation of an international currency that would not jeopardise the country's financial stability, the Chinese leadership followed a remarkably cautious approach, characterised by extreme gradualness. Perhaps never before, as in the case of currency policy and the management of the balance of payments capital account, has China lived up to the slogan launched by Deng Xiaoping in the 1980s more literally. "Cross the river by feeling the stones," that is, advance so slowly that one's feet, firmly anchored on the ground, can feel the effect of each step.

After much hesitation, Beijing now seems to have made the internationalisation of the "people's currency" an official policy objective and is now implementing a concerted strategy to realize this ambition. Indeed, the Chinese government appears determined to use all its capabilities to promote the renminbi's role as an international currency. Beijing's dirigiste and planning attitude seems to suggest great confidence in the possibility of designing an international currency by rolling out a "managed" internationalisation process on the supply side. According to John Cohen, "the yuan has embarked on a Long March to global status, reminiscent of the Long March that was instrumental in the Communist Party's victory in China's civil war. This is clearly a deliberate act, a deliberate attempt to influence the situation. The resources of power are being used instrumentally to expand the use of the renminbi abroad; wider use of the renminbi, in turn, should increase China's influence and prestige."

There are many observers today who believe that the renminbi will soon become a full-fledged international currency, accepted outside China to settle financial and commercial transactions, and also used as a billing and payment currency. In the words of the Indian economist Arvind Subramanian, the reasoning is that "China's growing economic size and dominance is also likely to translate into currency supremacy [...] The renminbi could overtake the dollar as the leading reserve currency even before the middle of this decade." The internationalisation of the renminbi is considered by many economists, policymakers, and fund managers to be China's next big thing in the world. This conviction stems from the fact that China has become a manufacturing and trading power in a short period of time, relative to the economic history of the world. Therefore it is bound to have a significant impact on the international monetary order as well. In John Cohen's view, however, this confidence, while apparently not entirely unreasonable, is not based on analyses of the conditions necessary for the widespread international use of the renminbi. Intead this stance stems more from considerations of the inevitability of the effect on economic processes – in this case on international financial markets – of the extensive network of economic transactions built up by China over the past four decades. If China has managed to become the key supplier of many crucial components of a large number of manufactured goods, and has shown determination in pro-growth economic reforms, why should it not be able to build a system that promotes the international use of the renminbi?

Bringing a currency like the renminbi, one of the most tightly controlled in the world, up to the level of the euro and the yen, not to mention the dollar, is a very different goal from the ones China has pursued so far. The main difference lies in the fact that this objective, unlike the others, cannot be achieved by intervening only inside the country, but requires an evolution of China's financial relations with foreign entities and subjects; and these relations, unlike those between the Chinese authorities and the Chinese government, cannot be managed by force. In order for foreigners to automatically start using the renminbi, it is not enough to aspire to global status for this currency, or simply declare the intention to promote its use across borders. One option to increase the international circulation of the renminbi is coercion. As Benjamin Cohen suggests, some degree of coercion might only be possible in Hong Kong, which is formally subject to mainland China's sovereignty, and perhaps even in some states such as North Korea. In this case the renminbi might be able to function in a way similar to what Susan Strange meant by the term "master currency" (Cohen, 2015). In fact, for the renminbi to become a true international currency (and not just be accepted as a billing and/or payment currency for import/export contracts with China), first there must be foreign demand. Then the Chinese authorities must be willing to meet this demand with an adequate supply of the currency. At the moment, neither of these conditions exist in the slightest, nor is there any sign of them emerging on the horizon. One of the essential conditions for the emergence of an international demand for renminbi is the existence, in addition to economic convenience, of a certain degree of trust in the issuing country. It is not a question of trust in political stability or in economic power, but of the trust of individual investors and of the financial markets.

Besides direct coercion, there are two ways in which Beijing is trying to foster the rise of the renminbi to international currency status. On the one hand, the Chinese authorities are leveraging the size and power of the Chinese economy to encourage its use in bilateral transactions with foreign countries, based on the assumption that it is cheap compared to any third-country currency, particularly the dollar. On the other hand, the international use of the renminbi is pursued through the coercive, albeit indirect, effect of China's great economic influence on the economies of many countries in the world, which translates into political power of persuasion.

One way or another, the renminbi should be made more attractive to potential users. At the moment, of all the factors contributing to the emergence of international demand for renminbi (other than that motivated by the need to regulate bilateral trade with China), it is the size of the Chinese economy, expected to become the world's largest in less than a decade, which is the most significant. By contrast, all other factors are almost completely negligible, including insufficient development of the domestic financial market.

For some years now, the Chinese government has been trying to achieve a managed internationalisation of the renminbi by leveraging convenience and persuasion, in two areas: foreign trade and finance. In foreign trade (as we shall see in Chapter 3), currency swap agreements have been initiated with foreign central banks to facilitate the use of the renminbi as a means of payment. On the surface, the contingent purpose of swap agreements is to insure against the kind of risks that might arise from another global financial crisis. Specifically, the availability of renminbi funding in a future crisis would insure Chinese trading partners against any future (dollar) liquidity crisis. But the currency swaps are also designed to provide renminbi for use in bilateral trade on a more regular basis, which represents an indirect incentive for the commercial use of the Chinese currency. In the private sector, regulations have gradually been relaxed since 2009 to allow more commercial transactions to be invoiced and paid for in renminbi, avoiding traditional invoicing currencies such as the dollar.

Besides international trade, the other area where the international use of the renminbi is being promoted is international finance. Markets for renminbi deposits and renminbi-denominated bonds, mainly "offshore" in Hong Kong, the former British Crown Colony that has been a "special administrative region" of China since 1997. As we shall see below, Hong Kong is a key component of the PRC's currency and financial strategy that has so far served as a financial firewall, allowing Beijing to remain effectively insulated from international financial instability, while having to move an immense amount of dollars from foreign trade payments on a daily basis.

The trade track has initially seen much more progress than the finance track, but the latter is gaining momentum. The renminbi's Long March began in late 2008, when the PBoC began negotiating a series of local currency swap agreements to provide renminbi financing to other central banks for use in trade with China when needed. Six years later, pacts had been signed with over twenty economies, including major players such as Argentina, Australia, Brazil, Britain, Indonesia, Russia, Singapore, South Korea, Switzerland and the United Arab Emirates. The size of the individual swaps varies widely, from just 700 million renminbi (about

$110 million) for Uzbekistan and 2 billion renminbi ($322 million) for Albania to 360 billion renminbi ($58 billion) for South Korea and 400 billion renminbi ($65 billion) for Hong Kong. Total facilities amount to about 2.7 trillion renminbi ($435 billion).

Billing in renminbi is gradually spreading, and the currency's use for trade purposes is expected to expand substantially in the years ahead. The results on the financial front, on the other hand, while not insignificant, have been less impressive. For the most part, Beijing has proceeded cautiously, relying heavily on Hong Kong's status as a special administrative region. With its own currency and financial markets, Hong Kong offers a useful offshore laboratory for testing innovations that the leadership is not yet ready to introduce "onshore" on the mainland. The model is unusual, to say the least. Never before has any government deliberately sought to develop an offshore market for its currency while maintaining strict financial control at home.

***

In order to assess the actual progress of renminbi internationalisation, it is useful, as suggested by Barry Eichengreen and Masahiro Kawai, to distinguish trends in renminbi usage into four areas: renminbi transaction settlement, renminbi-denominated investments, renminbi bond issuance and renminbi currency swaps, and direct trading. In particular, Chinese banks' renminbi settlement for cross-border trade peaked at 7.23 trillion renminbi in 2015 before falling to 5.23 trillion renminbi in 2016. The settlement of renminbi cross-border direct investment increased dramatically in 2015 before slowing down in 2016 (when the value reached 2.46 trillion, including 1.40 trillion of foreign direct investment). This reversal of renminbi internationalisation coincides with a slowdown in bilateral currency swap agreements. Indeed, the negotiation of bilateral swap agreements is one of the key means of securing adequate renminbi liquidity to cover an open position. Through these agreements, partner countries are able to obtain the renminbi needed by their domestic financial institutions. The guaranteed provision of renminbi liquidity allows foreign monetary authorities to authorise banks regulated by them to support renminbi exposures.

In the marathon to attract foreign investors, foreign ownership of Chinese bonds finally reached the 3% threshold in October 2020, up sharply from 2.6% in 2019. Net bond inflows to that date amounted to 807 billion renminbi, 76% higher than a year earlier. Although the share may seem modest, it indicates China's commitment to attracting foreign capital in a difficult geopolitical environment. The faster recovery from the Covid-19 pandemic in China sets the stage for positive growth in 2020, in contrast to the rest of the world. This growth divergence has resulted in a one-year government bond yield spread between China and the US of 260 basis points in October 2020, compared to 98 basis points in April 2020: an indicator of the potential for new investment opportunities, all the more so with a strong renminbi. Beyond yields, China offers a diversification option, as the correlation between Chinese and global bond yields is relatively limited. The inclusion of Chinese bonds in global indices has also helped to attract capital inflows.

On a less positive note, capital inflows into the Chinese bond market only go to the safest assets, namely Treasury Bonds and bonds of the development banks (China Development Bank, Agricultural Development Bank of China and Export-Import Bank of China). The share of foreign ownership in Chinese Treasury Bonds rose from 2.6% in 2015 to 9.5% in October 2020, approaching the 13% level seen in Japan and Korea. While there is room for growth in bank bonds, of which foreign investors hold only 5% of the total, it is crucial for China to attract capital in bonds issued by local governments, companies and banks. This serves not only to maintain the momentum of inflows, but also to reduce the high credit spreads between government and corporate bonds, especially for private companies. If the juicy spreads have not yet convinced investors, it is clear that further reforms are needed, in addition to opening up, to attract foreign inflows. These include improving disclosure, credit ratings, corporate governance and investor protection.

Future inflows into Chinese bond markets may grow at a slow pace as the renminbi has appreciated beyond what might be acceptable. The moves made by the PBoC to eliminate the reserve requirement for forward forex trading and the countercyclical factor are signs of concern with regard to a strong renminbi: more action could come if a one-way expectation builds. Indeed, with the current strength of the renminbi, investors may no longer feel comfortable maintaining large inflows to China.

***

To assess progress in the use and development of renminbi-denominated cross-border business and products, Asian Banker, together with China Construction Bank, launched the *Global Renminbi (RMB) Internationalisation Report*, which is based on a survey of 346 companies (230 in China and 116 overseas) and 52 financial institutions. The Report revealed growing optimism in renminbi internationalisation, particularly with the BRI. In 2017, there was a significant upsurge in the use of renminbi among respondents, higher in international payments by Chinese companies. The Report also found a strong interest in the Chinese onshore bond market by financial institutions, with the Chinese interbank bond market emerging as the preferred channel.

The survey also underscored an improvement in companies' overall confidence in the pace of renminbi internationalisation, i.e. the use of the currency for international transactions. Some 65% of firms said the pace had increased, while 25% of foreign firms said it had "increased significantly." The BRI initiative was found to be the most significant driver of renminbi internationalisation, as cited by 72% of respondents. This was followed by "the inclusion of the renminbi in the IMF's Special Drawing Rights (SDR) basket" (which we will discuss in more detail shortly), cited by 60% of respondents.

The impact of a more stable renminbi is evident. In fact, already in 2017, 46% of Chinese companies, 43% of foreign companies and 48% of financial intermediaries increased their use of the currency in international transactions. Among financial intermediaries, 63% showed interest in China's onshore bond market. As far as the channels used to access it, 52% of respondents said they preferred the interbank market, specifically using the China Interbank Bond Market, followed by the RMB Qualified Foreign Institutional Investor (RQFII) Scheme.

***

In the long run, the internationalisation of the renminbi could provide a useful tool for reducing dependence on the US dollar. The opinion of the Chinese elite has never been unanimous, not even after 2009, when, as one observer put it, "the Chinese government obviously changed its mind and became enthusiastic about renminbi internationalisation." On the one hand, there are the factions led by the PBoC that see internationalisation as a way to advance liberal financial reforms. On the other hand, firms are concerned that wider use of the renminbi could drive up its price, eroding export competitiveness. Banks and state-owned enterprises, which have long benefited from the government's tight controls on interest rates and credit allocation, also fear that an uptick in interest rates might follow a wider use of the renminbi. As a result of these divergences, no formal statement on internationalisation as official Chinese policy has ever been launched, although in fact Beijing has been progressing on its peculiar strategy to expand the international circulation of the renminbi and internationalisation has become "at the heart of China's financial strategy" by 2011.

At the 2020 Financial Street Forum in Beijing on 21 October, Zhou Xiaochuan, the former head of the PBoC, expressed his views on the short-term prospects for renminbi internationalisation. While the renminbi had recently appreciated significantly in the markets, Zhou said that this trend should not be overemphasised, as the currency had benefited from China being the first major economy to recover from the Covid-19 pandemic. China, Zhou said, was firmly pursuing the path of opening up to the outside world, both in the real economy, including through the creation of ports and free trade zones, and in the financial markets, through measures such as Shanghai-Hong Kong Connect, Shenzhen-Hong Kong Connect and Bond Connect. Zhou made it clear that China believed it could minimise capital account controls as much as possible, while protecting the country from the negative effects of uncontrolled capital flows. Zhou also said that further capital account convertibility did not necessarily mean "100% liberalisation," as all countries have anti-money laundering and anti-terrorism requirements, and many financial transactions and forms of remittances are subject to restrictions.

***

Beijing, in fact, has long since developed its own road map that depends on the Hong Kong Monetary Authority (HKMA) (Hong Kong's central bank and the head of the financial regulator) to act as its faithful representative. Back in 2004, the HKMA launched the renminbi Business Scheme, allowing Hong Kong banks to open renminbi deposit accounts for individuals and some businesses. But the offshore deposit market (informally known as the CNH market, as opposed to the onshore market, designated by the acronym CNY) did not start to take off until mid-2010, when new rules were issued easing restrictions on Hong Kong banks' renminbi assets. According to Benjamin Cohen (2016), daily trading of the renminbi on the Hong Kong foreign exchange market was allowed and local financial institutions were able to open renminbi accounts on their own account for the first time, paving the way for the creation of a wider range of tradable financial products, including exchange-traded funds and derivatives of various kinds. The result was rapid but still limited growth in the total value of CNH deposits, from less than 65 billion renminbi ($10 billion) in December 2009 to around 860 billion renminbi ($140 billion) at the end of 2013. Although nearly 150 licensed Hong Kong institutions now participate in the CNH market, the amounts involved remain minuscule by international standards to date.

In 2007 certain mainland banks were first allowed to raise funds by issuing renminbi bonds in Hong Kong, which started to develop an offshore market for renminbi-denominated bonds. The first so-called "dim sum" bond (a slang term taken from a popular cooking style and used to refer to a renminbi bond issued outside China) was issued by the China Development Bank in July 2007. However, progress in the market was slow, as mentioned, until 2010, when authorisation was extended first to non-financial Chinese enterprises and then to foreign multinationals doing business in China. Among the first non-Chinese companies to enter in June 2010 were the Hong Kong & Shanghai Banking Corporation (HSBC) and the Bank of East Asia, followed by big names such as McDonald's, Caterpillar, Volkswagen and Unilever. In the three years since, the market has more than tripled, with the value of new issues rising from just 40 billion renminbi ($6.3 billion) in 2010 and a cumulative total of just 22 billion renminbi ($3.3 billion) previously. In total, more than 360 dim sum bonds had been issued by the end of 2013. In early 2014, the International Finance Corporation, a subsidiary of the World Bank, sold a one billion renminbi ($163 million) bond in London, the first dim sum issue outside Hong Kong. The net outstanding volume increased nine-fold in five years, to around 580 billion renminbi ($92 billion) in 2015, and then to around 400 billion renminbi in 2018.

Parallel to the dim sum market, an onshore market for renminbi-denominated bonds, centred in Shanghai, has also been developed. The process began in 2005, when debt sales by non-Chinese issuers – known as "panda" bonds – were first allowed within China. Initially limited only to "eligible" multilateral development institutions, access to the panda bond market was expanded in 2009 to include subsidiaries of locally incorporated foreign multinationals. But new issuances remained few and far between, especially for state-owned financial institutions such as the Asian Development Bank, the Japan Bank for International Cooperation and the International Finance Corporation. 2010 saw the first sale by a private banking institution, Tokyo-Mitsubishi UFJ (China) Ltd; and in March 2014, German carmaker Daimler AG was the first foreign non-financial company to sell a panda bond, for about 500 million renminbi ($81 million). But these numbers are even more minuscule by international standards. Shanghai therefore still has a long way to go to fulfil the State Council's commitment. Here, however, progress has been particularly slow, even after the Chinese State Council's well-publicised commitment in 2009 to turn Shanghai into an international financial centre by 2020. Indeed, Shanghai has the most developed financial exchange in mainland China, foreign financial institutions have increased their presence in the city: in 2019, Shanghai attracted a record $19.05 billion in foreign capital, up more than 10% from the previous year. As a result, Shanghai was ranked the fourth most competitive financial centre worldwide, second only to Tokyo in Asia in the latest Global Financial Centres Index. Shanghai has a strategic location, as it offers access to markets in mainland China. It has become a financial hub for China, but is also a contender in the race to become an international financial hub, starting from the rest of the Asia-Pacific. In order for Shanghai to become an established financial hub for international transactions, along the lines that Hong Kong followed, the whole regulatory framework should be designed. This would include the rule of law, enforceability of contracts and, last but not least, the convertibility of the Chinese yuan, the lack of which imposes additional costs of doing business.

***

The Chinese economy has grown and will grow even more, eventually outsizing the United States, which has been the largest economy for at least a century. The volume of trade alone, however, will not be enough to increase the weight of the renminbi in international transactions. Despite its great weight in world trade, China today still has a small percentage of exports denominated in its own currency, and in this sense is very similar to post-World War II Japan. This is largely due to China's foreign trade structure, which has so far been characterised by a large share of intermediate goods compared to final goods being traded; in other words, it is strongly embedded in global value chains. With its low labour costs, China has become the "factory of the world," encouraging the import of high value-added inputs and components (e.g. computer chips) that can then be processed or assembled into final products for export. In such a network structure it makes sense to denominate all links in the value chain in a single, widely accepted international currency such as the dollar. This is not likely to change as soon as Beijing hopes, unless China succeeds with plans to move up the technology ladder to higher value-added industrial products, as it has already done in areas such as solar panels and wind turbines, and manufactures them with indigenous technology. And since throughout the industrial world exports of manufactured goods tend to be invoiced and settled in the exporter's currency, the more China is able to shift its production structure in this direction, the easier it will be to continue to grow the renminbi's role in international trade.

However, successfully augmenting the international use of the renminbi in trade transactions is challenging. One can expect Beijing to continue to try to exploit the advantage of its big role in global value chains. In essence, the leadership's idea is to leverage, as far as possible, the sheer size of "economic China," and the resulting incentive for trade partners to consider using the renminbi to settle trade transactions with China. In this sense, Beijing hopes that foreign traders will be willing to use the renminbi for the added financial and political convenience that this currency offers in engaging with an increasingly important trading partner. Many observers indeed think that the Chinese market has now grown so big and so crucial for many partner countries, that the latter tend to be inclined to place the need to secure market access before any other political consideration.

Not so long ago, as reported by Benjamin Cohen (2015), there was a consensus among informed observers, that reform of both domestic financial markets and external capital controls is essential for successful internationalisation. As Jeffrey Frankel, an economist at Harvard University, put it, "If China is not yet ready to liberalise its domestic financial markets [and] legalise capital inflows [...] then full internationalisation is probably a long way off." It certainly seemed a long way off in 2015, when Frankel was writing, but it no longer seems so today, just a few years later, when one considers China's plan to achieve managed internationalisation. Similar to the role of the renminbi as a trade currency, when it comes to the other critical roles that Beijing has included in its international financial strategy, namely the use of the renminbi as an investment vehicle and as a reserve currency, the economic dimension is becoming more and more crucial. It was suggested until recently that these are the roles that truly add value in terms of political power. These attributes are an advanced degree of financial development, providing the liquidity and predictability that market participants expect from a reserve currency, and a large, strong capital market, sufficiently open to outsiders, is an essential prerequisite that Beijing still lacks. Should we be surprised then to see how little progress has been made on the finance route in the Long March of the renminbi, as opposed to the trade route?

In this regard, a particularly tricky point is the question of renminbi convertibility. At the very least, convertibility for current account transactions seems to be an absolute requirement to sustain the internationalisation process. As the stories of the Deutsche mark and the yen show, widespread adoption of a currency for cross-border use is possible even in the presence of a substantial set of capital controls. Massive financial liberalisation began in Germany or Japan only long after their currencies had already gained widespread acceptance. This would seem to indicate that full convertibility of the renminbi is not at all necessary. But it is also clear that the performance of the mark and yen could have been even better if full convertibility had been introduced earlier. Some degree of internationalisation of the currency was sacrificed to maintain control on domestic financial stability.

This is the same dilemma China faces today. Some increase in capital convertibility would seem necessary if Beijing wants to increase interest in the renminbi as an investment vehicle or reserve asset. However, the degree of convertibility Chinese authorities are prepared to introduce is still not clear. At the very least, market participants and central banks should be free to open bank accounts in renminbi and to buy and sell certain classes of Chinese bonds and shares. Foreigners will not find renminbi-denominated credits attractive if the latter cannot be bought or sold at will. But at the same time, trading in certain classes of liquid credits – especially in more speculative areas such as options, futures or other exotic derivatives – could remain prohibited or tightly regulated in order to reduce the risk of destabilising capital flows.

Whatever degree of convertibility is allowed, however, there is clearly a need for further financial reform at home to make the renminbi attractive as a store of value. So far in the all-important bond sector, progress has been painfully slow in both the dim sum and "panda" markets. The large economic size of China, which is rapidly becoming the largest economy in the world, is not going to be enough to develop an unconditional willingness to accept the renminbi as a currency for transaction and as an asset denominating currency. Trust does not grow with GDP, but with the reliability and independence of a country's monetary authority, both of which are still not present in China.

***

One of the crucial factors China is leveraging to raise the renminbi's international status is its inclusion as the fifth currency (after the US dollar, the euro, the Japanese yen and the British pound) in the IMF's SDR basket on 1 October 2016. The IMF Board also decided that the weight of each currency would be 41.73% for the US dollar, 30.93% for the euro, 10.92% for the Chinese renminbi, 8.33% for the Japanese yen and 8.09% for the British pound, respectively. At the launch of the new composition, Christine Lagarde, the then IMF Managing Director, said that the expansion of the SDR basket would represent a historic moment for the Fund, for China and for the entire international monetary system: a significant change for the Fund, because it is the first time since the adoption of the euro that a currency has been added to the basket. The Board justified the decision by stating that the inclusion of the renminbi reflected the advances made in reforming China's monetary, currency and financial system, and by recognising the progress, albeit limited, made in liberalising and improving financial market infrastructure. Continuing and deepening these efforts, with appropriate safeguards, will lead to a more robust international monetary and financial system, which in turn will support growth and stability in China and the global economy.

In retrospect, the IMF's decision was not a trivial one, nor one with minor consequences for the international monetary system. First of all, with a weight of 10.92% in the total basket, the inclusion of the renminbi has the potential to make the value of the US dollar more volatile in the basket. Moreover, as analysed in an IMF study itself, historically, the renminbi has always been pegged to the dollar, so adding it to the basket can be seen as a similar effect to increasing the weight of the dollar, but if China continues on its path towards a more flexible exchange rate regime, this relationship will gradually change. But the most insidious consequences are probably the political ones: the inclusion of the renminbi has cleared Beijing's currency strategy, and with it perhaps its entire financial strategy, which aims to make the renminbi a currency with wide international circulation, but without being fully convertible.

The renminbi: an "unfinished" currency?

In the vast literature on the process of opening up and reforming the Chinese economy, the consensus is that the missing piece is still the financial one. China controls capital flows with the rest of the world, the value of the renminbi exchange rate and the huge amount of liquidity circulating within China's borders. The renminbi is a non-convertible currency (i.e. it cannot be freely exchanged with other world currencies); its international circulation is still restricted by the Chinese monetary authorities to the amount needed to settle commercial transactions, but the currency is not used as a form of financial capital (except to a small extent). Thus the use of the renminbi as a medium of exchange, unit of account and store of value is rather limited.

Even the inclusion of the renminbi in the IMF's SDR basket has not changed the situation radically. As we have just seen, the dollar's share in the basket is roughly four times larger than that of the renminbi, indicating that the Chinese currency is not yet a truly internationally-accepted currency. On the other hand, the symbolic and political value of the inclusion is something else entirely, as the Chinese authorities have interpreted it as a sort of official approval of the renminbi's internationalisation strategy adopted since 2009. This strategy does not envisage an unconditional liberalisation of capital movements or the exchange rate, which few of the attentive observers of Chinese economic policies have ever really expected, but an articulated system of "communicating vessels" of which China maintains careful control. As we shall see in this chapter, the Chinese plan to achieve a vast international circulation of the renminbi is complex, the fruit of a long-term vision and an articulated combination of pieces which, taken individually, do not have a particularly disruptive value, but put together constitute an ingenious plan.

China has always been very ambitious in choosing its development strategies and has long been trained to manage the complex monetary and currency policies needed to support these choices. First of all, in order to preserve the country's financial stability, the PRC's capital account is still almost completely closed, although there has been a slight opening since 2012. According to the capital account openness index calculated by the IMF (an index whose values range from 0 for maximum openness to 1 for maximum closure), the global average is around 0.4 and has changed very little between 2012 and 2017. Grouping the world's countries by level of income per capita, it can be seen that the degree of openness is significantly lower for the richest countries. High-income countries fell from 0.18 in 2012 to 0.21 in 2017; middle-income countries remained around 0.5 and low-income countries in the range of 0.7 to 0.66. In 2017, China had an index of 0.85, down only slightly from a value of 1 in 2012.

Maintaining capital controls and a controlled fluctuation exchange rate means that a major exporting country, as China has been for at least three decades, needs complex monetary and currency management. Indeed, China's high trade surplus since the 1980s has forced the PBoC to accumulate large dollar reserves on the one hand, and to continually put sizeable amounts of domestic currency into circulation on the other. At the same time, China keeps its exchange rate in a controlled fluctuation regime, at a level sufficient to preserve the tremendous price competitiveness that has enabled its goods to conquer world markets.

For a large exporting country, which receives a huge amount of foreign revenue on a daily basis, having a non-convertible currency means having to manage a mass of liquidity in dollars that exporting companies have to exchange for renminbi – once completely, now to a large extent (since it is possible to keep part of the export revenue in dollars to make payments abroad). Export earnings thus generate both massive currency reserves for the central bank and huge amounts of liquidity in renminbi. To prevent a continuous rise in currency in circulation from generating inflation at home, China's monetary authorities are forced to continually compensate for the increased liquidity from exports by issuing renminbi government bonds, with which they absorb the excess money in circulation (an operation known as *sterilisation of the monetary base*).

Because of its inconvertibility, the renminbi is considered an unfinished or immature currency, i.e. lacking the main functions that a national currency should have in order to be able to regulate international transactions. These functions are: to be a unit of account with which to express the price of national exports, and to be a medium of exchange with which to settle transactions operationally (mature currencies perform both these functions).

Not having a convertible currency therefore means that China's dependence on the dollar is twofold: financial and political. On the one hand, the accumulation of huge reserves in dollars, considered by many observers merely as a source of power vis-à-vis the issuing country, i.e. the United States, is in reality also a source of weakness or dependence on the politics of that country, since this state of affairs influences the interest rate and the exchange rate of the dollar, to which the renminbi is pegged. Moreover, of the entire mass of dollars in circulation in the world, which earns the US a seigniorage, the part that China keeps in the form of official reserves fluctuates in value according to the quotations of the dollar. For example, after the outbreak of the financial crisis of 2008-2009, the weakening of the dollar has triggered major risks for the value of China's foreign reserves: according to the estimates of the Bank for International Settlements, to an extent that could reach $1,800 billion (out of a total of $2,700 billion of reserves) in the event of an appreciation of the renminbi by 10%. But China's dependence on the dollar is also a political dependence: being tied to the dollar payment system dangerously exposes the country to the real risk of being cut off from that system in the event of further escalating tensions with the United States, and forces China to find ways to reduce its dependence on the dollar, which today represents more of a liability than an asset.

In order to downgrade this dependence, since 2009 the Chinese authorities have been designing a system that would allow a gradual uptick in the international circulation of the renminbi, without making it convertible. This has nothing to do with a generic internationalisation of the Chinese currency, understood as the liberalisation of capital movements and the exchange rate. On the contrary, the aim of the Chinese authorities is to channel the renminbi into the wallets of international investors and those who use it for international payments, by creating offshore centres for the currency. In this way, assuming that demand for the renminbi escalates, the Chinese monetary authorities will be able to meet the needs of that demand and drive it up, without jeopardising the country's financial stability by unconditionally opening up financial flows and capital movements.

***

Today, the completion of the BRI represents a great opportunity to proceed along the path of this particular strategy of internationalisation of the renminbi, i.e. expanding its international circulation, while at the same time not allowing its value be freely determined by the currency market. The proper functioning of the BRI requires, as a necessary element, the ability to price and settle supply contracts for materials in renminbi, to provide loans in renminbi to finance infrastructure construction projects abroad, and to be able to conclude e-commerce contracts with foreign countries in renminbi: all of which drive up foreign demand for renminbi and thus promote its greater internationalisation.

Why the Chinese authorities have planned such a complex system, as we shall see in this chapter, depends on their desire to maintain control over the fundamental monetary variables – the interest rate, the inflation rate, the exchange rate. At the same time they are freeing themselves from dependence on the dollar, by creating a vast regional area of circulation of the renminbi in Asia, with a series of outposts in all other parts of the world. As we saw in Chapter 1, China has decided nothing less than to openly challenge, in a rather original way, the recognized goal and mutual irreconcilability of three contextual monetary policy objectives: free international capital mobility, a stable exchange rate and monetary autonomy.

The long hand of Chinese foreign loans

Over the past two decades, to be precise between 1998 and 2018, China has become the world's largest official creditor, surpassing even the IMF and the World Bank: China's direct loans and trade credits to the rest of the world have risen from almost zero to more than $1,600 billion, or nearly 2% of global GDP. Most of these loans go to low- and middle-income countries, with the PRC now accounting for a quarter of total bank lending to emerging markets. China's presence is even more significant in poor countries, where it has overtaken not only private creditors, but also multilateral creditors such as the IMF and the World Bank. What has made China such a large global creditor over the past two decades is the dramatic upsurge in China's GDP, combined with the Going Global or Go Out policy, initiated in 1999 and aimed at promoting Chinese investment abroad, as we have seen.

***

With respect to China's entry into the international financial system at the beginning of the 21st century, there is a major gap in the academic literature: there is almost no research on the consequences of China's global "financial shock," whereas China's "trade shock" has been widely studied. As a result, while China's role in world trade is well known, the rise of Chinese capital exports to the rest of the world in recent decades and its expanding role in global finance is poorly documented or understood.

Little is known about these loans. First, China does not disclose its official loans and there is no comprehensive standardised data on the stocks and flows of Chinese debt and loans abroad. As reported by Horn and colleagues (Horn et al., 2019), credit rating agencies, such as Moody's and Standard and Poor's, monitor sovereign loans from private creditors (banks, bondholders or others), but sovereign loans to countries (i.e. state-to-state) are off their radar. The Paris Club is the institution that monitors sovereign lending by sovereign creditors, which in principle should cover most of China's overseas lending, but China is not a member of the Club and therefore not subject to the disclosure requirements that apply to member countries. Overall, the record on Chinese capital exports is opaque to say the least.

In addition to the scarcity of data, commercial providers such as Bloomberg or Dealogic do not track Chinese official borrowing abroad. For its part, the PBoC does not publish its sovereign bond purchases or the composition of its portfolio. Moreover, China does not provide sufficient details on its direct lending activities to the BIS, nor does it disclose data on its official flows to the OECD Creditor Reporting System. Finally it is not a member of the OECD Export Credit Group, which provides data on long and short-term trade credit flows.

As regards cross-border banking, according to Horn and colleagues (2019) China has only recently joined the list of countries reporting to the Bank for International Settlements (BIS), but data are not made available on a bilateral basis and coverage is incomplete. These limitations in information hinder rigorous empirical work on China's official capital exports, at least until 2019. This is the year of publication of the thorough study on Chinese international lending by Horn and colleagues, based on a database covering 1974 Chinese loans and 2947 Chinese grants to 152 emerging and developing countries, from 1949 to 2017 (Horn et al., 2019). This study highlights the many unresolved problems so far in trying to understand China's role in contemporary international finance. The first is the so-called "watertight compartments" as labelled in the literature, due to the fact that the various relevant strands of research have remained largely disconnected from each other. Many aspects are studied, but each is analysed individually. There is also the topic of central bank reserve accumulation and capital flows from emerging to advanced countries, which shows that China is a major buyer of bonds issued by advanced countries. Other widely studied topics are China's foreign direct investment and equity investments in advanced countries, and capital flows from China to developing countries, notably through aid, grants and loans. Although each of these strands of investigation sheds light on the components of China's official capital outflows, none of them provides complete data on China's international capital exports. These include portfolio investments, purchase of productive assets, cross-border bank loans and trade credits, through to official loans between governments and between central banks.

According to Horn and colleagues (2019), today's data show that the PRC has always been a very active international lender, even in the 1950s and 1960s, when it lent substantial amounts to allied communist states despite severe hardship and famine. Just as the post-World War II Marshall Plan was certainly not yield-seeking, so today China's official flows do not necessarily reflect the yield-seeking incentives of private agents, but are shaped by the geopolitical objectives of the Chinese government. Overseas lending declined in the 1980s and 1990s, but picked up again in the early 2000s as China's economy boomed and its share of global GDP is now more than 15% .

China's foreign loans also have many characteristics that differentiate it from lending by other sovereign creditors. First, while in recent decades sovereign creditors have typically lent to developing countries on concessional terms with long maturities and below-market interest rates, China has instead often granted (and continues to grant) loans on market terms (with risk premiums), shorter maturities, and partly with collateral clauses that guarantee repayment through revenues from commodity exports, particularly oil. (We will explore this further in Chapter 3.) According to Horn and colleagues (2019), such practices have a historical precedent: China's foreign lending shares several features with 19th century French, German and British foreign loans, but were not entirely market-based. Another important historical precedent is the lending boom of the 1970s, when resource-rich and low-income countries received large amounts of syndicated bank loans while commodity prices soared. China's lending flows in 2008-2015 bear similarities to this lending cycle, which ended unhappily once commodity prices, export earnings and economic growth collapsed in many of the debtor countries (indeed, after 1982 dozens of countries in Latin America and elsewhere went into default, resulting in a "lost decade"). A new wave of over-indebtedness by many countries seems on the rise, if one considers the sharp rise in the incidence of Chinese sovereign debt restructurings since 2011. Concerns about debt sustainability mainly involve developing countries that have received the most Chinese loans. Many of them have benefited from the Heavily Indebted Poor Countries (HIPC) debt relief initiative, and debt levels and debt service burdens in more than 20 developing countries are already much higher than previously thought.

Looking at the global position of China's foreign loans, it is evident that China tailors its overseas lending according to the recipient. Rather than direct loans, advanced and upper-middle-income countries receive portfolio investments, through the PBoC's purchase of sovereign bonds. According to Horn and colleagues (2019), many advanced countries have become heavily indebted to the Chinese government. In particular, Chinese purchases of US Treasury bonds (and other US fixed-income assets) have skyrocketed since the early 2000s, reaching a peak of $1.6 trillion in 2011, equivalent to 10% of the US GDP. Treasury data on foreign purchases of US assets make it easier to monitor this type of bilateral lending. However, the PBoC has also stepped up its purchases of other countries' sovereign bonds over the past decade, and these asset purchases, as noted above, are more difficult to track. Other types of government financing, notably officially guaranteed trade credits and flows of equity and foreign direct investment to advanced countries, have also grown strongly.

As for China's total foreign loans (combining direct investment, trade credit and direct loans), their sum, as a percentage of global GDP, skyrocketed between 1998 and 2019, from just over zero (almost all export credit) to around 1.7% (more than half of which is trade credit, followed by direct loans, while foreign direct investment is relatively small). In 2018, the Chinese government held more than $5 trillion in debt to the rest of the world (6% of global GDP), compared to less than $500 billion in the early 2000s (1% of global GDP). Adding in foreign equity and direct investment, China's total financial claims abroad amounted to more than 8% of global GDP in 2017. This marked increase in Chinese official lending and investment is almost unprecedented in peacetime history, being comparable only to the escalation of US lending in the wake of World War I and World War II. Indeed, rapid credit growth has turned the Chinese government into the world's largest sovereign creditor (the number one overall creditor, adding sovereign and private credits, remains the United States). Despite these developments, however, we know surprisingly little about Chinese capital exports and their global implications.

Along with the increased outflows, the geographical scope of Chinese lending has also expanded significantly. The share of countries receiving official Chinese grants or loans has exploded since 2017 to nearly 80%. With almost full global coverage, US official loans are still larger than Chinese official loans, but the gap is rapidly closing. The overseas lending boom has turned China into one of the world's largest official creditors, especially to low-income countries, where Chinese loan flows have exceeded total capital flows from multilateral creditors such as the IMF or World Bank, as well as flows from private creditors.

According to Horn and colleagues (2019), we need to consider another type of capital export, i.e. equity investment, or direct foreign investment and Chinese holdings abroad. In this case we can refer to data published by the American Enterprise Institute and Heritage Foundation (more accurate than the official statistics published by the Chinese Ministry of Commerce, which do not adequately capture China's large foreign direct investment flows through offshore financial centres, in particular via Hong Kong). This source together with IMF data show that these two types of flows tend to be directed mostly to the same set of countries.

The main recipients of outward foreign direct investment from China include European countries (Italy, Greece, Scandinavia, Germany, and the UK), as well as a variety of African, Asian and Latin American countries. For developing countries, there is a high correlation between foreign direct investment flows and direct loan flows, leading to a scenario of high financial dependence of many countries, which could also result in excessive political dependence.

***

It is clear, therefore, that over the last two decades China has become a dominant player in the international financial system. The size, characteristics and direction of China's capital exports to the rest of the world suggest that about half of its large-scale lending to developing countries remains "hidden," i.e. unaccounted for in the major international databases used by researchers and practitioners. According to Horn and colleagues (2019), these hidden foreign debts pose serious challenges to country risk analysis and bond pricing. Debt sustainability metrics are therefore less reliable than generally perceived, especially with regard to some developing countries that borrowed heavily from China during the boom decade of 2003-2013. However, advanced countries have also progressively indebted themselves to China, mainly through PBoC sovereign bond purchases and other foreign direct investment debts.

In short, the global financial landscape has changed considerably over the past two decades, as China has emerged as a global economic powerhouse not only in trade but also in capital exports. In the post-World War II Bretton Woods era, global capital flows were largely dominated by sovereign flows, mainly from the United States. The dismantling of capital account restrictions in advanced economies following the collapse of Bretton Woods ushered in a new era of private capital flows in international finance. The 1970s and 1980s were characterised by international syndicated bank lending, while in the 1990s bond and equity flows replaced bank lending. Today the sheer volume of Chinese official borrowing abroad makes it necessary to incorporate China as a relatively new but systemically important creditor. Currency swap agreements, in particular, give rise to what might be called China's financial outposts in the world. Although taken individually they do not constitute true innovations, taken together they are a precursor to something much more impressive: an ambitious and innovative strategy to internationalise the renminbi.

China's financial outposts in the world

Probably the least known of all forms of Chinese lending abroad are the large-scale swap lines arranged between the PBoC and some foreign central banks. Swap lines are permanent lines of credit between central banks and thus another form of official financing. Of course, this does not change cross-border flows unless the line is activated.

After the 2008 global financial crisis, the PBoC greatly expanded its network of currency swap lines, first with central banks in advanced countries and then including selected emerging and developing countries. In total, as of 2018, China has signed swap agreements with over forty foreign central banks for a total of $550 billion. According to the aforementioned study by Horn and colleagues, in terms of geographical scope, this is by far the largest swap network of any central bank in the world. According to McDowell (2019), currency swap arrangements are not new to the world of central banking. The US Federal Reserve (FED) pioneered the technique back in the 1960s and maintained permanent lines with a group of major central banks for several decades until the late 1990s. After a brief resurgence following the terrorist attacks of 11 September 2001, it was in 2008-2009, during the worst months of the Great Financial Crisis, that the Fed famously relied on such arrangements to provide liquidity abroad. Since 2008, swap agreements have become increasingly popular among emerging markets, with China being by far the most active player.

When a currency swap line is activated, both parties agree to exchange their currency, or a hard currency such as the dollar (drawing on their foreign exchange reserves), for the other party's currency. McDowell (2019) explains that such agreements usually set limits on the size of the transaction (i.e. how much can be exchanged) and its duration (i.e. when the exchange should be reciprocal, i.e. when the central banks will have to exchange the same amount of currency at the exchange rate of the initial transaction). Although both banks purchase foreign currency when the swap lines are activated, generally one party is the borrower (the party requesting the activation) while the other is the creditor (the party accepting the request). For the duration of the swap, the creditor holds the acquired foreign currency, while the borrower uses the acquired funds to meet its financial needs. Thus, although with a somewhat more complicated mechanism, currency swaps function as loan guarantees. And this is also true of China swaps. However, unlike the Fed's swap lines, the PBoC's swap programme is designed to provide central bank partners with liquidity in renminbi rather than dollars.

In the midst of the 2009 global financial crisis, Zhou Xiaochuan (then governor of the PBoC) expressed his scepticism about the desirability of having an international monetary architecture based on a single, super-sovereign reserve currency. Indeed, the dollar shortage not only reduced trade with the US, but also restricted transactions between China and other countries, since the US dollar is the main currency for international transactions.

Since the first bilateral currency swap line agreement was signed in December 2008, 32 have been opened. One notable case dates back to October 2010, when Hong Kong drew 20 billion renminbi to meet the territory's trade financing needs. In 2013, Korea accessed 62 million renminbi, while in 2014 China tapped 400 million Korean won through its bilateral local currency swap agreement to facilitate foreign trade financing. Argentina, instead of using it to settle trade, drew on the swap line with China in October 2014 to deal with the collapse of its foreign reserves. According to a 2015 PBoC report, total use of these swap lines amounted to 96.5 billion renminbi at the end of 2014.

These swaps aim to support trade and investment and promote the international use of the renminbi. As China limits the amount of renminbi available to settle trade, the swaps were used to obtain renminbi once the ceiling was reached. The PBoC does not publish detailed data on the use of its swap lines, but from information compiled by the Currency Swap Agreement Tracker by the Council for Foreign Relations, it is possible to reconstruct a geographical overview of China's swap line network as of 2018. Moreover, it is possible to deduce the outstanding claims of the swap lines by inspecting the balance sheets of the recipient central banks. This exercise (carried out again by Horn and colleagues' 2019 study) indicates that since 2013 Pakistan, Argentina, Mongolia and Russia have used their standing lines with the PBoC to curb market pressures and to strengthen foreign exchange reserves. In contrast, the most recent data indicate that China currently has outstanding claims on only one country – Argentina, which initially drew about $10.5 billion from the PBoC. After an agreement to expand the swap line to $18.7 billion at the end of 2018, Argentina's central bank debt to China likely augmented further.

***

The boom in currency swap agreements began with the great global financial crisis of 2008-2009, when the international monetary system experienced a severe liquidity crisis (i.e. a shortage of dollars in circulation, the so-called "dollar squeeze"); this severely curtailed global trade and put pressure on international banking activities. The US authorities, in response to the high global market stress, have since set up dollar swap lines with major central banks to mitigate the global pressure on their currency. On 31 October 2013, a network of central banks comprising the Bank of Canada, the Bank of England, the Bank of Japan, the European Central Bank, the Fed and the Swiss National Bank agreed to activate a bilateral liquidity swap with the United States.

The dollar squeeze irrefutably highlighted the danger of operating in a global context centred on the US financial system. And so it was in 2009 that China committed to implementing measures to promote the cross-border use of the renminbi and reduce its dependence on the US dollar, a move that was seen by the international community as a clear signal of China's intention to internationalise the renminbi. In the same year, China also launched a programme to encourage the denomination and settlement of its international trade in renminbi. The latter measure resolved a practical issue in China's foreign trade, namely the currency's limited availability outside the country's borders. Indeed, China at that time had much stricter rules on the movement of the renminbi across borders. So at this point, in order to facilitate the renminbi trade settlement initiative, China signed the first bilateral currency swap agreement with the Korean central bank in December 2008. The second was signed with Hong Kong in January 2009. Since then, China has signed swap agreements with economies around the world.

In 2000, China joined the Chiang Mai Initiative (CMI) – a regional network of multilateral currency swap agreements among the ten members of the Association of Southeast Asian Nations (ASEAN). The agreement with Korea was not part of a broader multilateral framework like the CMI, but it was bilateral. Moreover, the swap was not created to make dollar liquidity available between banks but instead the transaction between Beijing and Seoul was specifically designed to function as a liquidity pool between banks for their respective domestic currency markets – in this case, the renminbi and the Korean won.

In the decade afetr, the PBoC expanded its currency swap network. Today, Beijing has opened more such agreements than any other central bank at any time in history. Taken together, these currency swaps with central banks on every continent amount to nearly 500 billion renminbi available to China's foreign partners – a sum almost equal to the IMF's total resources.

China expanded its swaps since 2008 at an unprecedented pace, which makes the overall currency swap network take a much broader significance.

China's currency swaps can be seen as financial statecraft on the part of the PBoC. As Saori Armijo and Leslie Elliott Katada argue, a country's financial or monetary capabilities are used to achieve foreign policy objectives. Although not a novel expression in the field of international political economy, "financial statecraft" has recently started to attract scholarly attention. Most often associated with the sanctions literature, its meaning has expanded to encompass any policy aimed at influencing international politics through capital flows. Of course, this meaning could include punitive measures, such as sanctions, but also friendly measures, such as the financial rescue of foreign governments. In short, as discussed by McDowell (2019), the art of finance can be used offensively (as a "sword") or defensively (as a "shield"). Distinguishing offensive from defensive use is the fact that the former aims at strengthening the influence of one state over others, while the latter seeks to preserve the autonomy of a state from foreign influence. China has used swaps for both purposes.

On the defensive side, swaps are designed to promote the use of the renminbi as a currency to settle trade transactions, thereby reducing China's dependence on the dollar for its foreign liquidity requirements. Yet the PBoC's swap network has so far done little to reduce China's dependence on the US currency. Indeed, although the use of the renminbi in foreign trade contracts saw an upturn from 2009 to 2014, it has since declined and most Chinese trade continues to be settled in dollars. Moreover, only some of the swaps have been activated for the purpose of settling international trade transactions.

As regards the offensive side of financial statecraft, swap transactions can be used to offset short-term liquidity shortages outside the Bretton Woods institutions for partner countries facing difficult financial situations. The ability to act as an international lender of last resort on behalf of foreign governments would help China improve its global status, to the extent that it would enhance Beijing's international influence and contrast the ability of the United States to apply sanctions to foreign governments in the form of constraints on their dollar operations. While examples are still few, some swap lines have indeed been used for such purposes since 2014. Recently, Russian foreign minister Lavrov suggested that Russia and China should increase the renminbi sphere of their foreign transactions, so as to reduce the dollar share and therefore the amount of transactions on which sanctions could be applied. This is the biggest potential challenge of currency swaps to the global economic order.

***

From the outset, bilateral currency swap agreements have become a key feature of China's efforts to promote the use of its currency abroad. In addition to its application to regulate trade transactions, the swap line is perceived as a liquidity tool for offshore trading, which serves to ensure the stability of renminbi markets outside national borders. Compared to the US swap lines set up during the global financial crisis, these Chinese swap lines are not just for hard times, but instead are a part of a more general policy of integrating the renminbi and the Chinese financial sector into the global financial market.

The swap agreement exemplifies China's view of its role in the international monetary system. With this in mind, it is interesting to ask what empirical factors determine the establishment of bilateral currency swap agreements. According to Lin and colleagues (2016), a number of studies have analysed how commercial activity has influenced the formulation of China's bilateral currency swap agreements, concluding that the swap agreements, like all of China's other economic agreements with the rest of the world, were not necessarily driven by purely economic considerations. In fact, non-economic factors, including political relations and societal institutional characteristics, play a major role in determining Chinese currency swaps. In particular, the research shows that the decision to establish a Chinese bilateral local currency swap line depends on economic factors, political considerations and institutional characteristics, including, for example, trade intensity, economic size, strategic partnership, and free trade agreements. Once the decision for a currency swap arrangement is made, the size of the line is mainly influenced by trade intensity, economic size and the presence or absence of a free trade agreement.

Although the frequency and volume of use so far is relatively low, the interest in establishing bilateral local currency swaps with China is supported by bilateral trade opportunities and by the prospect of being part of China's major currency globalisation programme especially after the introduction of the e-CNY. Along with the initiative to promote the use of the renminbi in commerce, China has gradually opened up its financial sector and encouraged the use of the renminbi abroad in both commercial and financial transactions. For example, offshore renminbi markets, which originated in Hong Kong, have spread to different time zones and continents, with an increasing number of renminbi-denominated assets. Therefore, the currency swap arrangement "defines a specific and managed channel through which the renminbi is made available abroad; however, it has become part of China's policy of promoting the offshore uses of its currency" (Lin et al., 2016).

In addition to the designated function of providing liquidity to ensure the smooth functioning of offshore renminbi markets, bilateral currency swap agreements are seen as a symbol of approval and support for renminbi activity abroad, and signify trust between sovereign authorities. Therefore, the motivation for setting up a swap agreement is driven by both economic and political considerations.

Initially, currency swap agreements had a strong concentration in Asia-Pacific and Central Asia, then spread to other geographical areas. Moreover, among the partner countries a large proportion are emerging and developing economies. The observations corroborate the view that China is adopting a regional approach to establish its global economic network. Typically, these agreements last for three years and are renewed upon expiry. So far, only Belarus and Uzbekistan have not renewed their swap agreements.

Despite China's continued efforts to liberalise its financial markets, conversion between offshore and onshore renminbi is typically conducted within designated channels, including free trade zones, the RQFII programme and licensed renminbi clearing banks abroad. Thus, bilateral currency swap agreements will continue to promote the global use of the renminbi both as a symbol of the approval of offshore renminbi assets in the partner market and as a back-up liquidity line for the renminbi.

***

Recently, a number of studies have questioned the implications of the internationalisation of the renminbi with regard to economic integration between China and its partners, particularly its partners in the BRI. While at an intuitive level it is easy to argue that economic integration brings with it the need to use an international currency, thus stimulating the internationalisation of the currency, there are still few empirical studies that rigorously address the issue.

Chey, Kim and Lee (2019) found a significant impact on a state's interest in using the renminbi stemming from its institutional economic cooperation with China through a preferential trade agreement or bilateral investment treaty. Other scholars have specifically explored the role of bilateral currency swaps on the evolution of bilateral trade flows between China and its partner countries. The data show a significant and positive effect of such agreements on trade, with a 30.4% improvement in bilateral trade between China and its partners; for BRI countries, this effect is even more pronounced, reaching 37.3%. The most interesting result is that the BRI effect is separate from the positive impact of reduced exchange rate fluctuations, which usually favour bilateral trade. Among the 35 economies that have currency swaps with China, more than half belong to the BRI, and among the 68 BRI countries, more than one-third have signed bilateral swap agreements with China. Therefore we can say that the BRI countries are also important partners of China in the renminbi internationalisation process.

Another interesting result is that a country's negotiation of swap agreements had a significant positive effect on trade flows both before the great financial crisis and afterwards. Indeed, pre-crisis agreements contributed to improvements in bilateral trade flows with signatory countries of up to 108% more than flows with countries that were not signatories to swap agreements; this effect after the crisis appears more modest, but still shows improvements of as much as 40%. For China, on the other hand, the effect of swap agreements on trade flows is not so high: before the financial crisis, swaps between China and its partners (all of which are covered by the CMI) did not generate a significant effect on trade flows. After the financial crisis, on the other hand, the effect of swap agreements on trade flows was more significant, with trade flows improving on average by 28.5% compared to those of non-signatories. Moreover, such agreements within the MIC had no decisive effect on trade flows (indeed their effect was even negative), whereas swaps after entry into the MIC began to have a positive effect on trade flows.

Hong Kong: still a financial firewall for China?

While the decisive role played by Hong Kong so far in China's growth experience is unanimously acknowledged, there is much less agreement on Hong Kong's position and function in China's current growth strategy and its future place in the country's opening trajectory. For some years there has been a lively academic debate about whether and why China still needs Hong Kong, with widely divergent positions. This debate has been partly inspired by the series of political protests that have taken place in Hong Kong since 2014, movements whose origin and interpretation are closely linked to the evolving relationship between mainland China and the special administrative region which is what Hong Kong has been for more than two decades. Added fuel for the debate, perhaps not coincidentally in the same years, comes from the renewed vigour of China's policies of openness through international trade and foreign direct investment, already evident in the past but now cleverly organised within the BRI.

In this section we will briefly look at the channels (finance, trade, rule of law) through which China's economic growth strategy has been and continues to be centred on Hong Kong, and then try to disentangle the bewildering divergence of views on Hong Kong's relative importance to mainland China today. We will focus on several aspects of Hong Kong's changing role, which is still essential to China's very particular strategy of openness to date, though no longer to the extent that it has been in the past. We will see that Hong Kong is and will continue to be very relevant to China's future "opening up," but it will also be destined to lose its unique position. In fact, Beijing has diluted its functions as a financial hub and extended them to a range of other locations outside its borders through the so-called financial pillar of the BRI, while at the same time incorporating the benefits of its commercial and legal status into mainland China through the Greater Bay Area.

***

Within the enormous body of economic literature on how China has integrated into the world economy by extending its participation in global trade, finance and investment networks over the past four decades, Hong Kong is recognised not only as an important part, but also as the most decisive one. This does not mean that all the unprecedented economic achievements of the People's Republic of China have been possible only because of Hong Kong's role, but that the region has made these achievements possible in the specific way in which they have been realised.

First, Hong Kong has been essential to the inflow and outflow of international direct investment into and out of China, and has proved a very powerful engine for China's growth through massive learning and technological spillovers to domestic enterprises. Hong Kong has always been and still is a pivot for China's foreign direct investment, both inbound and outbound. Although the share of inward FDI into Mainland China through Hong Kong has declined over time, due to lower barriers for companies to invest directly in China, outward FDI from China still benefits from Hong Kong's efficient regulatory environment and professional services that encourage ventures into foreign markets. As for outbound foreign direct investment from China, according to the Ministry of Commerce of China (MOFCOM), in 2018, more than 58% (about $70 billion) of the flows went to Hong Kong; as a result, at the end of 2018, the stock of Chinese foreign direct investment in Hong Kong reached $622 billion.

In terms of international trade, after four decades of selective opening policies, in 2013, just twelve years after joining the World Trade Organisation, China became the world's largest exporter (in goods, not so in service exports, where the United States ranks first). Due to Hong Kong's special customs administration, the amount transiting through the SAR has gradually decreased since China joined the World Trade Organisation in 2001, but the same cannot be said for Hong Kong's role as a facilitator of trade links between China and the rest of the world. This was made possible by a development model that promoted cheap exports so as to earn enough foreign exchange (dollars) to pay for imported technology, machinery and industrial inputs which China once had insufficient skills and production capacity to manufacture domestically. The key to a massive upsurge in exports was the ability to manage the exchange rate so as to prevent it from appreciating: as demand for Chinese goods from around the world increased, appreciation would indeed be the inevitable fate of the renminbi, but this would gradually erode Chinese price competitiveness. For China, therefore, exchange rate management has been key to becoming a major exporting nation.

***

In the economic history of the world all great trading nations have had international currencies. Within the British Empire the pound sterling was used in all international transactions and to regulate international trade, so the pound sterling remained the world's main trading and reserve currency as long as the British economy remained at the centre of the global economy, both for manufacturing and finance. When Britain was overtaken by the United States in economic size, industrial capacity and trading power, the pound was downgraded from an international to a domestic currency, while the US dollar became the main international currency, both for trade and reserves. Today, the renminbi is still not convertible, not yet traded internationally, nor is it used as a reserve currency, although, as we have seen, in December 2015 it was included in the basket of currencies that make up SDRs at the IMF. All international transactions with China as a partner have been and still are mostly carried out in dollars.

For China, the possibility of becoming a major trading nation without an international currency has largely relied on Hong Kong's role as an offshore centre, both for trade settlement and for the international circulation of the renminbi. To understand this, one has to consider that the costs to China of running a huge trade surplus in dollars have been enormous. The rapid accumulation of dollars from export earnings, while keeping the exchange rate under floating control, required extensive sterilisation by the PBoC (i.e. the central bank had to buy huge amounts of dollars in exchange for renminbi and then issue renminbi-denominated bonds to avoid an excessive buildup in the money supply at home).

In order to cut these substantial macroeconomic costs, China has started to reduce its dependence on the dollar as a trading currency on the one hand, and the cross-border circulation of the renminbi on the other. However, the monetary authorities in mainland China did not want to run the risk of financial instability that would go hand in hand with a traditional currency liberalisation. Nor did they want to let the renminbi exchange rate fluctuate in the currency markets. Two intervention schemes were devised to meet these requirements: a renminbi cross-border trade settlement scheme, to amplify the use of the local currency as a trading currency; and the opening up of an offshore renminbi market, with the aim of boosting the cross-border use of the local currency. The first is a mechanism to use the renminbi in import payments through an authorised bank in Hong Kong; launched in 2009, the purpose of the scheme was improving trading conditions by providing liquidity in renminbi at a time when the financial crisis had reduced liquidity for commercial transactions. The initiative was primarily and initially intended to settle trade contracts with neighbouring countries. The second is a market for renminbi and renminbi-denominated assets outside mainland China, which was launched in 2007 with the dual aim of allowing Chinese companies investing abroad to raise funds in the capital markets, and for non-Chinese to hold renminbi assets. The offshore circulating renminbi (CNH) was convertible into foreign currency, unlike the onshore renminbi (CNY).

Hong Kong has been central to both schemes. Hong Kong's unique status served as a buffer between the Chinese and international markets in the so-called "two-tier" or "two-track" strategy to multiply the international circulation of the renminbi, without liberalising the capital account by making the renminbi convertible. It is true that the PRC has become the largest trading nation in the world and the number two economy by GDP, while Hong Kong now accounts for 3% of China's economic size compared to 16% in 1997. But is also undoubtedly true that the mainland has managed to handle such a massive amount of trade transactions without a convertible currency precisely because of the two intervention schemes just described, both centred on Hong Kong. The offshore renminbi market has allowed Chinese state-owned enterprises to list shares and raise funds in Hong Kong, which is the most developed offshore market for renminbi-denominated bonds, the so-called "dim sum" market (to distinguish it, as explained at the beginning of this chapter, from the onshore bond market, the so-called "panda" market). Hong Kong, for its part, is still the main offshore renminbi market, with the largest offshore liquidity pool outside mainland China.

In short, this approach has allowed China to interact with international currency and financial markets through a kind of "financial firewall," protecting the domestic market from the potential instability of a liberalised capital account. As a result, China's share of global equity and debt markets has increased significantly. At the end of 2018, China's bond market accounted for 12.6% of the global total, up from 1.2% in 2004. In comparison, in 2018 the US, EU and Japan accounted for 40.2%, 20.9% and 12.2% respectively, all down from 2004 when they represented 42.2%, 26.5% and 18.7% respectively.

Finally, while it is true that Hong Kong has acted as a buffer between China and international markets, due to its unique position the region has been facing intensifying competition from other offshore renminbi markets, and is therefore losing strength compared to the past. This explains why current views on whether China still needs Hong Kong span the extremes of a very divergent range of positions.

***

When we understand the broad outlines of Hong Kong's essential role in China's past growth, and the specific channels and mechanisms through which mainland China has benefited from such a special offshore financial centre, we can re-interpret the recent debate on whether Hong Kong is still as important today as it once was.

The two most representative positions, at opposite ends of this debate, are well summarised by two op-eds. According to Eswar Prasad, one of the staunchest advocates of the decline of Hong Kong's special economic and financial status, China's economy and financial markets have expanded so rapidly that Hong Kong's relative size is much smaller than in the past, not in absolute terms but only in relative terms. (In 2018, the value of Hong Kong's new public listings was higher than any other stock exchange in the world.) But Prasad goes further than those who believe that Hong Kong's relative importance has diminished. And he points to two developments. One is the changing willingness of foreign companies and investors to deal with the Chinese mainland, regardless of "shortcomings in its corporate and public governance," with an eye to benefiting from its growing market potential. The second development is an attempt by Beijing to promote Shanghai as an international financial centre, thus creating a rivalry between the two centres. By allowing Shanghai to trade in renminbi and renminbi-denominated assets with offshore centres, Hong Kong's once unique status will be lost. Hence the conclusion that China no longer needs Hong Kong as it once did. Moreover, by anticipating the end of the special status in 2047, the central government would have "imagined an entirely different purpose for Hong Kong, [...] to show the effectiveness of China's version of the rule of law, where the legal system serves the economy by enforcing property and contractual rights, but is ultimately subservient to the Communist Party."

While many other proponents of the view of Hong Kong as now irrelevant to China fall into the fallacy of absolute size, Prasad emphasises Hong Kong's still central function to China. This hardly correlates with its economic size in terms of GDP, but does with the amount of international trade and financial flows between China and the rest of the world that travel through Hong Kong. With regard to these flows, China still relies heavily on Hong Kong as a financial centre, but it is seeking to scale down its financial dependence on Hong Kong by creating more offshore financial centres to manage renminbi liquidity abroad. These other centres are effectively competing with Hong Kong, thus threatening the unique status it had until now. However, no other centre in mainland China is in a position to compete with Hong Kong, not even Shanghai or Shenzhen. Although it can leverage its economic size and financial ties to attract economic activity and listed companies, Shanghai simply does not possess the essential elements that make Hong Kong unique, a wide-ranging set of characteristics including financial power and infrastructure, rule of law, efficient bureaucracy and regulatory framework, trade and logistical capacity. Critics of Hong Kong's financial importance to China therefore tend to overemphasise the ability of other offshore centres to replace Hong Kong and eventually push it out of its monopoly position.

At the other end of the debate, proponents of Hong Kong's continued centrality to China emphasise the uniqueness of such a comprehensive offshore centre, which has no counterpart in mainland China. This view is effectively presented by Tianlei Huang who elaborates on Hong

Kong's function as a market capitalist centre that allows mainland China to leverage its rule of law while keeping the situation stable at home.

One of the most important reasons why Hong Kong still maintains a crucial role for China is its system of registered initial public offerings (IPOs), compared to the more cumbersome and arbitrary approval system of mainland China. According to the China Securities Regulatory Commission (CSRC), "Shanghai has started testing IPO registration, but it is not yet known when all listings on the Shanghai and Shenzhen stock exchanges will become registration-based." A large number of Chinese state-owned enterprises (SOEs) rely on the Hong Kong Stock Exchange (SEHK) to either have their headquarters directly there or to locate a subsidiary that is listed on the SEHK. According to the World Economic Forum, this system has been crucial for Chinese SOEs to circumvent the approval system on the mainland and even more so to gain access to one of the world's leading stock exchanges in the world's freest economy for twenty-five consecutive years since 1995.

The SEHK allows capital to be raised for a vast number of Chinese companies (both incorporated in the mainland and incorporated abroad but controlled by Chinese entities), including SOEs, bypassing the widespread condition of financial repression in the mainland. According to HKEX Group data, more than 30% of SEHK's total market capitalisation was accounted for by Chinese companies at the end of February 2020, up from 16% in 1997. However, it is also true that the share of Chinese companies in SEHK's total market capitalisation climbed steadily for the first decade to over 51% in 2008, to then descend. This is probably the result of a decline in the importance of SEHK for Chinese companies, coinciding with the emergence of a number of competing centres for raising capital, notably Shanghai and Shenzen.

***

In the summer of 2020, China celebrated the first anniversary of the Shanghai Stock Exchange (SSE) Science and Technology Innovation Council, more commonly known as the STAR Market. This is a new stock exchange that, since its inception, has aimed to create a viable competitor to the US Nasdaq and a good alternative for technology companies looking to file an IPO in a hub other than the US or the Hong Kong Stock Exchange. The surprising performance of the STAR market in its first year of operation exceeded all expectations, reaching the second place in the global IPO ranking in 2019, behind Nasdaq and ahead of Hong Kong. This can be attributed to government reforms introduced to speed up the IPO process through a market-driven registration mechanism, while lowering barriers to entry and multiplying funding opportunities for technology companies.

But Shanghai will not be alone in offering a viable platform for technology companies. In fact, ChiNext, the technology board of the Shenzhen Stock Exchange, valued at around $1 trillion in market capitalisation, is introducing similar reforms that will amount to a serious challenge in Shanghai to attract the future listing of the most innovative domestic technology companies. In particular, ChiNext is set to double its daily trading range, and companies will be able to oscillate by up to 20% on a daily basis compared to the previous 10% limit No restrictions on trading volume will be imposed on the first five trading days. Beijing FengShangShiJi Culture Media and Yangling Metron New Matter are among a batch of eighteen companies that have seized the opportunity offered by this noteworthy reform.

The decision to introduce innovative domestic trade reforms is a demonstration of China's plan to advance the development of its financial market. And by redoubling its efforts to further expand liberalisation policies to Shenzhen's Nasdaq-style technology board, China aims to create a competitive environment with Shanghai that can capture the growth of a sizeable number of domestic startups and unicorns that are increasingly in need of funding to develop their businesses.

In addition, the new policies also target Chinese companies that have operations in mainland China but are based in Hong Kong, the so-called "red chip companies." In other times, these companies would almost certainly have filed an IPO in the United States. But due to the introduction of anti-China IPO rules in the US, there is now an unprecedented opportunity for Shanghai and Shenzhen to attract domestic companies while helping to expand the size of the Chinese capital market.

By enhancing STAR Market and ChiNext, China is providing a safe haven for those Chinese technology companies that are no longer welcome in the US and are looking for a place to file a secondary listing. This also shows that China is navigating wisely as the US seeks to implement financial and technological decoupling. Moreover, intensifying domestic competition, although it will dilute Shanghai's share in this market segment, will lead to more efficient allocation of financial resources and higher valuation of technology companies that prefer to list closer to home, where most of their customers are located. This scenario will also attract the attention of global institutional investors who are always looking for high-yielding stocks to add to their portfolios. This has already happened in part, for example with the establishment of joint investment funds between China and other countries. In late 2019, Bank of China and Amundi, Europe's leading asset management company and a subsidiary of Crédit Agricole, announced the first asset management joint venture under the asset management framework regulated by the China Banking and Insurance Regulatory Commission (CBIRC) in the second half of 2020, with the majority stake held by a foreign shareholder. The joint venture between Amundi and BoC Wealth Management, the subsidiary of Bank of China, was approved by the CBIRC with the intention of demonstrating that the Chinese financial market is rapidly opening up.

***

In the context of China's opening-up policies, Hong Kong's role is still a very prominent one. However, precisely because it is so crucial, a number of challenges will emerge for China in the medium and long term. The special position of Hong Kong is linked to the status of the SAR, which according to the Joint Declaration between Britain and the People's Republic of China will expire in 2047. In light of this, in 1997 Beijing already began to prepare for the time when the "one country, two systems" model would no longer be based on that Declaration. This matter has become even more urgent because of the recent waves of social unrest in Hong Kong, which are largely related to the widespread perception and sentiment among Hong Kongers about Beijing's intent to phase out the unique features of the SAR.

The downgrading of Hong Kong's role as the main offshore centre for the mainland is achieved in two ways. The first is to start incorporating Hong Kong into the mainland so as to link and transfer its comparative advantage to the PRC or at least a part of this advantage. China is doing this through the mechanism of Special Free Areas, notably the GBA (we mentioned this at the end of Chapter 1), the scene of a new development framework planned from 2017 onwards on an expanded area around the

Pearl River Delta. Eleven metropolies on 56,000 square kilometres, with 70 million inhabitants, and a gross domestic product of over $1,500 billion. The aim is to take the area of Hong Kong, Macao and nine cities in the southern province of Guangdong (Guangzhou, Shenzhen, Zhuhai, Zhongshan, Jiangmen, Zhaoqing, Foshan, Dongguan and Huizhou), which taken together already contribute 12% of China's GDP, and turn this entire region into the world leader in terms of technological patents, start-ups, investments in innovative companies and digitalisation. Beijing wants to transform this collection of cities, businesses, startups, finance and infrastructure in the next Silicon Valley. The GBA project follows a three-pronged development strategy: alongside a strictly economic growth dimension and a political control objective, technological innovation is the third primary objective on which it is based. Beijing wants to open up the Guangzhou-Shenzhen-Hong Kong-Macao corridor to innovation, leveraging policies that promote the exchange of talent, capital, information and technology to create a large regional data centre. The hope is that the massive GBA project will help China gradually align its legal and regulatory regime with global standards for trade, finance, taxation and other transactions, while maintaining financial stability ensured by a closed capital account.

The second way to prepare for 2047 is to undermine Hong Kong's comparative advantages by expanding and enhancing the functions of other centres to compete with Hong Kong. This is done under the so-called financial pillar of the BRI, which includes the creation of a number of offshore clearing centres, none of which is fully comparable to Hong Kong, but each of which gets a slice of the offshore renminbi. These centres have expanded the range of markets that act as a buffer between the domestic and international markets. As of today, the main instrument has been, as we have seen, currency swap agreements between the PBoC and central banks in other countries.

The purpose of the two-pronged approach is to internalise the comparative advantages of Hong Kong's efficient free market system as far as possible into the mainland's system of financial repression and closed capital account, while at the same time diluting Hong Kong's financial and regulatory power by creating many more offshore centres. Such an ambitious strategy also brings with it a number of challenges. First, in order to remain a major trading nation without an international currency, China must find ways to augment the international use of the renminbi (which is quite different from advancing the internationalisation of the renminbi). According to the IDB, in 2019 the renminbi accounted for only 2.1% of total daily global foreign exchange trading – far below the dollar (44%), the euro (16%) and the yen (8.5%). Second, China will also need to have a more balanced current account, after decades of huge trade surpluses. An excessive surplus will require gigantic efforts to be governed with a managed floating exchange rate system, and in Beijing's eyes this surplus is too closely tied to the dollar system.

Overall, how well Beijing succeeds in implementing this plan will largely determine whether China can navigate international markets while maintaining strong control over the economy through a model that will conceivably move away from the "one country, two systems" to a "one country, two systems."

The e-RMB: China's great financial leap into the 21st century

In August 2020, the PBoC announced that it was about to officially launch a digital currency, the e-RMB (as it is called). In large cities such as Shenzhen the salaries of some civil servants and public services are partly paid with this virtual money and employees of state banks have begun testing the application internally to transfer money and make payments.

Anticipated for the end of 2019, the creation of a digital currency has been on Beijing's agenda for some time: at least since 2014, when the central bank set up a research team to explore the possibility. The e-RMB would have to be deposited in a digital wallet (e.g. in a mobile device) instead of a bank account, to replace traditional currency (i.e. renminbi notes and coins), and transactions would have to be made between two digital wallets without involving banks or credit cards. As 80% of mobile phone users in China today already pay with their devices, the e-RMB could reach 225 million Chinese who do not have bank accounts and live mostly in rural areas, where it could help boost domestic consumption. Mobile purchases in China already account for 16% of GDP (compared to 1% in the US and the UK) and could increment further as e-money becomes more widespread.

From an organisational perspective, China's planned financial architecture for issuing a digital sovereign currency has three levels: the central bank at the top, China's state-owned banks (which dominate the banking system and thus act as the operational arm of the central bank) at the second level, and consumers and commercial users who transact in e-RMB at the third level. China's major commercial banks, all of which are state-owned and operated, are conducting large-scale internal testing of a digital wallet application, in line with a target set by the PBoC for the second half of 2020. In April 2020, the e-RMB development institute at the PBoC announced closed internal trials of a Digital Currency/Electronic Payment (DC/EP) system in four cities and plans to pilot such a system in future Winter Olympics venues. Since then, as mentioned above, there has been a partial launch in a few cities: Shenzhen, Suzhou (for transport allowances) and Chengdu; Xiong'an, which is located south of Beijing and will host the Winter Olympics in 2022, is currently testing food and retail purchases and aims for a full launch at the international games.

The e-RMB represents a crucial step in China's financial strategy. It provides an ingenious solution to the many problems arising from a financial and currency policy that is focused on maintaining a high degree of control over international capital movements. It also reduces the cost of paper money circulation and tightens policymakers' control of the money supply. Prior to the initiative of a state-run e-RMB, the initial push for digital payments was motivated by the ease of online shopping by tech giants, such as Alibaba's Alipay and Tencent's WeChat Pay. Since the largest denomination of renminbi notes is 100 (i.e. about $14), physical currency is too small and inconvenient for high-value items. During the Covid-19 pandemic in particular, digital transactions were preferred to minimise risk of contact and contagion. From the perspective of policy-makers, digital payment can help deter fraud, corruption and (rampant) counterfeiting of banknotes.

The implications of the introduction of electronic money are both national and international. On the one hand, Beijing has long been concerned about the monopoly of digital money by technology giants and its impact on the financial system, as it falls outside the supervision of the central bank. In 2013, a fund offered through Alipay, Yu'E Bao, was so popular that it became the world's largest money fund in a matter of days, setting off alarm bells at the PBoC about the speed and scale of money drainage from China's bank deposit system. The central bank eventually intervened to limit the fund. In terms of external implications, the biggest, and perhaps most important, objective of the e-RMB could be a boost to the internationalisation of the renminbi, which has stalled since the China-US trade war began in 2018. The slowdown is most evident in the renminbi's trade settlement and the use of the renminbi in the BRI project.

The US policy of isolating China is a signal for the latter to seek alternative financing outside the US capital markets and in particular the dollar. The direct response is the strengthening of the renminbi capital market and the internationalisation of the local currency. If Chinese banks are banned from the global dollar transaction system (SWIFT CODE), the e-RMB has the potential to help the country's globalisation, but it could also pose a real challenge to the dollar as the world's reserve currency. A Chinese tourist, for example, with e-RMB could stay in an overseas hotel if the hotel had installed an e-RMB machine that makes transactions directly using the PBoC settlement system.

China's balance of payments flow could also be automatically and accurately monitored, and potentially grow much faster among emerging markets such as Africa, Latin America, Asia and the Middle East, with which China already has close economic, trade and strategic ties. The same argument can be extended to countries that, for example, face economic sanctions from the United States on dollar transactions. These countries could circumvent US surveillance of financial flows by transacting via e-RMB once the country has become part of a global network. China could use its electronic currency to build global strategic alliances against the US policy of isolation.

All in all, many observers fear that the growing tensions between China and the US could extend from a trade war to financial and technological conflicts. China's ambitious e-RMB plan could further amplify the impact of the tension by dividing the global economy into currency "zones." The e-RMB could also challenge Alipay and WeChat Pay (as they are still backed by bank accounts and credit cards) and other cryptocurrencies (at least in China), as the latter lack legal status and central bank balance sheet support.

Also, in August 2020 came the news that several Chinese commercial lenders, including Minsheng Bank, Guangfa Bank, Ping An, Shanghai Pudong Development Bank and China Merchants Bank, would launch American Express cards, which can now be used to settle bills in Chinese renminbi both inside and outside China. This is a drastic change from the previous rules that only allowed offshore card transactions to be settled in foreign currency. The news follows the recent clearance in June 2020 of the joint venture between American Express and Lianlian DigiTech Co. Ltd (the Express (Hangzhou) Technology Services Co.) to start credit card clearing services on mainland China (i.e. the process of transferring a transaction – its data and amount – from the financial institution that manages the agreements with merchants accepting the cards to the bank managing the credit card). In this way, the American multinational financial services company has opened the first foreign payments network authorised to carry out transactions in local currency in a market valued at $27 trillion in terms of mobile transactions.

The urgency of decisions in this direction stems from the real risk for China and its companies of being cut off from the dollar payment system in the event of further escalating tensions with the United States. There seems to be no alternative but to find ways of reducing dependence on the dollar, which is now more of a liability than an asset. By allowing foreign companies to operate in Chinese currency inside and outside the country, China's ultimate goal is to integrate its domestic payment services, still largely dominated by local players such as UnionPay International, Alibaba Group's Alipay, and Tencent's WeChat Pay, with the global financial system. In addition to this, the country seeks to promote a global renminbi clearing and settlement system that could eventually support trade and investment transactions between China and the rest of the world.

The PBoC's decision on American Express should not be an exception, but the start of a real opening process, as the other two major global credit card companies are also about to come on board. In fact, Mastercard has already received approval for credit card clearing operations in mainland China and Visa has applied and is currently awaiting approval. In this sense, the Chinese regulator's decision is strategically important because it sends a clear signal to the market: despite the ever-increasing tensions that characterise relations with the US, China is not prepared to adopt any retaliation against the business of American companies. On the contrary, the aim is to further elevate the global relevance of its huge financial market, on the one hand by providing greater access to foreign companies that could possibly augment the sophistication and expertise of the Chinese market, while at the same time promoting the internationalisation of the renminbi.

The decision to allow American Express to transact in renminbi both inside and outside China, coupled with the cooperation between the US company and China's leading mobile wallet providers, will be very welcome news. This is true both for Chinese tourists who will be able to make payments in their own currency abroad using the familiar ecosystems they normally use at home, and to foreign tourists who, when visiting China, will be able to rely on a digital wallet for their day-to-day transactions without having to deal with the complexity of exchanging cash on arrival and departure. In addition, the ability to leverage the extensive international cross-border network of American Express cards around the world, which in the US itself accounts for nearly a quarter of all credit card transactions, will serve as a springboard for the further use of the renminbi well beyond the BRI's borders and thus help support the internationalisation process.

China's decision to give US companies greater access to its clearing network can also be read through a political lens. In addition to the wider circulation of renminbi abroad that will ultimately strengthen the country's role in global finance, the true ultimate goal of opening up this network is reducing China's dependence on the dollar payment system while hedging against the unpredictable risk of receiving financial sanctions similar to those imposed on Russia, Iran, the Democratic People's Republic of Korea and Venezuela. In this regard, the Nikkei Asian Review reported that China is reportedly working with Russia to lessen its dependence on the dollar, in a move billed as a "financial alliance." In the first half of 2020 alone this strategy shrunk the dollar's share of trade between the two countries to below 50% for the first time, with the euro and their respective national currencies rising. This alliance is intended to respond to the US leading role in global finance, which is based on the dollar's status as the world's reserve currency and absolute control of the messaging system operated by SWIFT (Society for Worldwide Interbank Financial Telecommunication, based in Belgium). This gives Washington the ability to monitor every global transaction and unilaterally impose sanctions on countries and companies that use the dollar in their transactions.

In 2015, China also launched a China International Payments System (CIPS), a financial messaging network for cross-border transactions between mainland China and the two SARs (Hong Kong and Macao), which is also useful in the effort to internationalise the use of the renminbi. However, it will not be easy to abandon the SWIFT system, which is accepted worldwide, and such a move will probably only be part of a longer-term plan.

So the domestic market is opening to foreign credit card companies allowing bill payments in renminbi onshore and offshore, making the Chinese currency more widely traded in international transactions. Added to this is the continued development of the digital financial infrastructure and the expansion of pilot tests for a government-backed cross-border e-RMB payment system. All these decisions, while seeking to influence the dominance of the dollar, will help China emerge as a major global financial power.

3 The Renminbi as an Instrument of Soft Power

Historically, having an international currency has helped countries project their power and develop spheres of influence far afield. The United Kingdom and the United States, in the 19th and 20th centuries respectively, demonstrated how an international currency could help finance costly wars and economic interventions around the world. Financial power and political strength are closely intertwined. In the first two decades of the 21st century, China has managed to achieve many important milestones, mainly by leveraging its economic and demographic size. It now accounts for a huge share of the world economy – almost 20% of global GDP in 2020 – and is a key player in a vast area of economic interdependence that includes most countries around the globe. These achievements include becoming the largest exporter and the largest creditor to emerging and developing countries, even more so than the IMF and the World Bank. While these are substantial, other achievements are symbolic, including the inclusion of the renminbi in the IMF's list of international reserve currencies. However, to date the renminbi is not a true reserve currency in international markets, a status that can only be earned on the ground and not through formal decisions. For this reason, China has long pursued the goal of expanding the circulation of its currency across borders to the point of creating a parallel area to that of the dollar. This objective is to be understood not so much as a liberalisation of the Chinese currency market, i.e. a progressive loosening of controls on the exchange rate and on capital movements, but rather as an increase in the international circulation of the renminbi, without prejudice to the controls on the exchange rate and on capital flows. To this end, China has devised a very sophisticated network of agreements, institutions and financial transactions with a large number of countries, through which the renminbi is used as a tool to persuade, convince, attract and co-opt other countries to use the Chinese currency. In so doing the renminbi becomes a real vehicle of soft power, not only financial but also political.

The use of the renminbi as an international invoicing currency

To make the renminbi a truly global currency, China needs to expand the possibility to use this currency for invoicing and payment in international trade. Since 2009, Beijing has accelerated the process of promoting cross-border trade in Chinese currency with the Cross-Border Trade Settlement Pilot Project (SPR). This is a practical way to further boost international trade by helping Chinese exporters and importers reduce transaction costs and minimise the exchange rate risks associated with using the dollar. Expanding the currency's circulation and acceptance in foreign markets would, in turn, support its wider utilization in outward investment.

Through the SPR, Beijing initially allowed selected companies in five major cities in China (Shanghai, Guangzhou, Zuhai, Shenzhen and Dongguan) to invoice and settle their business transactions in renminbi, with Hong Kong, Macao and ASEAN countries. Beijing later lifted the restrictions and allowed all importers and exporters based in China to settle their trade transactions in renminbi. This policy triggered an upsurge in the use of the renminbi in trade, which almost tripled between 2009 and 2015, reaching a value of 7,200 billion renminbi.

At that time, and in line with Deng Xiaoping's thinking in favour of gradual, pragmatic and shrewd internationalisation, Beijing was interested in targeting mainly ASEAN economies rather than the world as a whole. Economic relations with these countries were set to grow rapidly thanks to the China-ASEAN Free Trade Agreement. According to a recent IMF study, so far that strategy has only partially borne fruit, as the renminbi's geographical area of influence remains limited to BRICS countries, no Asian renminbi bloc exists, and the dollar continues to play the main role.

The benefits of these policies are nevertheless visible, as highlighted by the OECD: the share of Chinese goods shipped abroad and priced in renminbi has now reached 30% (these are goods mainly destined for neighbouring East Asian countries), compared to 70% still in dollars, while no Chinese exports are denominated in euros. However, the use of the renminbi to settle commercial transactions is still mainly limited to Chinese companies. Following the devaluation of the renminbi, engineered by the PBoC in 2015, the process of internationalisation of the national currency has actually reversed somewhat in recent years: the amount of cross-border trade settled in renminbi has fallen to around 15% of the total, from a peak of 30% that year. Globally in 2016, the renminbi was used in just 1.7% of foreign currency-denominated transactions; in 2015, that share was 2.3%, a rather low figure considering that Chinese exports then accounted for around 10% of world trade.

Today, there are two developments that will have a positive effect on the use of the renminbi as a currency in international trade: through the BRI, China is lobbying for the renminbi to be used 1) for cross-border trade with partner countries through cash management, and 2) for financing and investment purposes at all different project stages.

In this regard, one of the most disruptive alliances on the currency front is between China and Russia, two countries which have recently begun to work together to reduce their dependence on the dollar – a development that some experts believe could lead to a true "financial alliance" between them. Indeed, there is already talk of a "de-dollarisation" phenomenon that is leading to a "turning point." In recent years, Russia and China have in fact drastically cut back on the use of the dollar in bilateral trade, but still in 2015, 90% of bilateral transactions were carried out in dollars. However, after the outbreak of the trade war between the United States and China and the concerted push by Moscow and Beijing to abandon the dollar, the figure dropped to 51% in 2019. In the first quarter of 2020, according to data from the Central Bank and the Russian Federal Customs Service, the dollar's share of trade between the two countries fell below 50% for the first time, while the dollar was used for only 46% of payments between them. At the same time, the euro reached an all-time high of 30%, while the respective national currencies accounted for 24%, also a new high.

De-dollarisation has been a priority for Russia and China since 2014, when they began expanding economic cooperation following Moscow's estrangement from the West over the economic and political consequences of the annexation of Crimea. At the time, the substitution of the dollar in commercial transactions had become a necessity to circumvent US sanctions against Russia, but today a banking and financial alliance, on par with or perhaps more than a military or trade alliance, is what can guarantee independence for both countries. Every commercial transaction that takes place in the world and involves the US dollar must at some point be authorised through a US bank, which puts the counterparts at risk that the US government may prevent certain transactions from taking place. In this sense, reducing the use of the dollar as a currency used in payments insures against the risk of sanctions by the US. The de-dollarisation process gained further momentum in 2018 after the Trump administration imposed tariffs on hundreds of billions of dollars of Chinese goods.

This process has also been facilitated since 2014 by a three-year bilateral currency swap agreement worth 150 billion renminbi ($24.5 billion), which allowed China and Russia to access each other's currency without having to buy it on the foreign exchange market. The agreement was extended for three years in 2017. Another crucial milestone came during Chinese President Xi's visit to Russia in June 2019, when Moscow and Beijing concluded a formal agreement to replace the dollar with national currencies for bilateral trade transactions. That agreement also calls for the two countries to develop alternative payment mechanisms to the US-dominated SWIFT network to handle trade in rubles and renminbi.

In addition to trading in domestic currencies, Russia has been rapidly accumulating renminbi reserves to the detriment of the dollar. In early 2019, Russia's central bank said it had cut its dollar reserves by $101 billion, representing more than half of its dollar assets. One of the biggest beneficiaries of this move was the renminbi itself, which saw its share of Russian foreign exchange reserves rise from 5% to 15% after the central bank invested $44 billion in the Chinese currency. As a result of this move, Russia has acquired a quarter of the world's renminbi reserves. Finally, in early 2020, the Kremlin granted Russia's sovereign wealth fund permission to start investing in renminbi and Chinese government bonds.

Russia's push to accumulate renminbi is not just about diversifying its foreign exchange reserves. Moscow also wants to encourage Beijing to become more assertive in challenging Washington's global economic leadership. But dethroning the dollar will not be easy. According to Jeffery Frankel, the dollar has three major advantages: its ability to maintain its value over time (as it has limited inflation and depreciation), the size of the US domestic economy, and the advanced, liquid, and open financial markets of the United States. So far, no rival currency has proved capable of outperforming the dollar on all three fronts. Yet Frankel himself also recognises that, while the dollar's position is secure for now, the debt spiral and an overly aggressive US sanctions policy could erode its supremacy in the long run.

The renminbi in commodities trading

One of the most important markets in which China is seeking to augment the use of the renminbi is the commodities market. China has long been the world's largest producer, consumer and importer of raw materials, but so far, its volume advantage has not been able to significantly influence the price of raw materials. Contracts for the purchase of commodities are concluded well in advance of the physical availability of these goods. These agreements are called futures contracts, whereby an obligation is undertaken to exchange a pre-determined quantity of commodities on a pre-determined date and at a pre-determined price, set on the date of the trade. Despite its great weight in many of these markets, China still suffers from the lack of a sufficiently developed domestic commodity futures market.

Commodity prices are mainly determined in North America and Europe, while in China, the Dalian Commodity Exchange (DCE), considered the world's second largest exchange for agricultural futures trading, has been operating since 1993. It is worth mentioning that futures trading also magnifies the volatility of commodity prices, due to the increasingly financial nature of this activity, where speculative factors in international commodity prices exacerbate their already high international fluctuation. This is why China, which is a major importer of many commodities, is particularly interested in boosting its pricing power.

If a country has the capacity to set the international price of raw materials its bargaining power is high. Generally speaking, international pricing power encompasses three abilities: to influence the price of international trade contracts; to impact international benchmark prices within the framework of existing rules; and to change existing international pricing rules. In fact, the United States has largely dominated the pricing of most commodities, because the US commodity futures market developed first, driving coverage of every sector. Therefore, the dollar has become the pricing currency for all commodities worldwide.

For example, prices of base metals such as copper, aluminium, lead, zinc, tin, nickel, are mainly quoted on the London Metal Exchange (LME); soybeans, corn, wheat and other agricultural products are linked to the Chicago Board of Trade (CBOT); prices of crude oil and other energy products depend mainly on the New York Mercantile Exchange (NYMEX) and so on.

The futures market in China has grown rapidly in recent years, paving the way for the denomination and settlement of spot commodity prices in renminbi. Currently, China's financial market consists of three commodity exchanges and a financial futures market, in which there are a total of 46 categories of commodities. In particular, Shanghai Futures Exchange (SHFE), Dalian Commodity Exchange (DCE), Zhengzhou Commodity Exchange (ZCE) and China Financial Futures Exchange (CFFEX) have 12, 16 and 2 categories respectively, which include energy and chemical products, agriculture, forestry, animal and fishery products, metal ores, rare metals and financial products.

China's commodity futures market was closed to foreign traders until the launch of the new crude oil futures in March 2018, when individual foreign investors were able to directly participate in a renminbi-denominated commodity futures market for the first time. However, lesser known to the world, products such as iron ore and purified terephthalic acid (PTA) were later opened to foreign investors as part of the government's broader plan to internationalise commodity futures markets. By the end of 2021, foreign investors are likely to have access to more than ten commodity futures contracts. Internationalized commodities in 2018 are: crude oil (March), iron ore (May), PTA (November). Other internationalised products include TSR 20 rubber (August 2019) and low sulphur fuel oil (June 2020). Products under discussion include methanol, soybeans, palm oil, copper, aluminium, nickel, zinc, lead and tin.

The first tangible signs of a shift to non-dollar quoted prices are already visible in the oil trade, where Beijing and Riyadh have strengthened bilateral ties. Saudi Arabia (the world's largest oil exporter) is expected to soon start accepting the renminbi as payment for its oil exports, usually denominated in dollars, to China (the world's largest oil importer), similar to oil companies in Russia, Iran and Venezuela. The renminbi-denominated crude contract also provided Iran with an easy way to circumvent US sanctions, which are usually applied when banks try to cancel dollar-denominated transactions – regardless of the counterparty's position.

There are several reasons why Chinese market participants want a renminbi-denominated benchmark in oil trading. In 2017, China overtook the United States as the world's largest net importer of crude oil, with oil consumption expected to reach $10 trillion a day by 2023. Trading on the new renminbi-denominated stock exchange allows Chinese importers to hedge their local currency in dollars, euros, yen or even gold through a variety of financial instruments created to allow this flexibility. In addition, the seven types of medium and heavy sour crude (mainly from the Persian Gulf) included in the benchmark are more representative of those used by refiners in China and other countries in the region, compared to the lighter, sweeter Brent (extracted from the North Sea) and West Texas Intermediate (WTI, extracted from the United States). Therefore, the price set in Shanghai is more representative of actual local market conditions.

Although the exchange is mostly used by domestic clients, international traders should be encouraged to take advantage of the hedging and arbitrage opportunities it offers to ensure adequate liquidity. To this end, the Chinese government has offered tax exemptions (for three years) and the relaxation of certain capital controls for foreign investors trading the new futures contract to encourage participation and generate liquidity. While trading volumes for this contract remain low compared to the Brent and WTI benchmarks (which is understandable as the product has just been launched), trading activity has picked up considerably in recent months.

A few days after the launch of the oil futures contract in Shanghai on 4 May 2020, China opened foreign trade in crude iron futures on DCE. However, unlike oil derivatives, the crude iron future launched in 2013 already serves as a benchmark for spot prices. More global traders on DCE should lead to more efficient pricing and greater liquidity. Unlike oil, gold and copper, for which prices are set in London and New York, iron ore is one of the few commodities whose global price is set in China. In 2017, Dalian's iron ore volumes reached almost 33 billion tonnes (in terms of contracts traded), compared to annual global trade of around 1.5 billion tonnes (in raw material).

In future, China will open up the possibility of trading a wider range of commodity futures to foreign operators. The London Metal Exchange is planning to introduce renminbi-denominated metal products, a sign that the currency's status in international finance is on the rise. In iron ore, Brazilian mining giant Vale was the first foreign trader in its sector to sign a contract with a Chinese steelmaker based on iron ore futures at the ECD, according to the exchange's website. While Beijing's consumption of oil and iron ore is a sizeable share of the global total, China also has enormous bargaining power in many other markets, such as aluminium, nickel, copper, zinc and steel.

Yet despite its position as a buyer on global markets, China is still primarily a price-taker that relies on foreign exchanges to price its goods and settles transactions almost entirely in dollars.

***

The commodities market is also the focus of the Chinese authorities' attention with regard to their foreign lending to developing countries. Many Chinese loans abroad are in fact repaid with or guaranteed by natural resources: some estimates suggest that between 29% and 32% of the loans granted between 2000 and 2014 were covered by some kind of commodity, usually but not exclusively oil. Others suggest that of the $132 billion in loans to African and Latin American governments between 2003 and 2011, more than half, or $75 billion, was in the form of loans secured by the natural resources exported by recipient countries, including oil, cocoa, platinum and diamonds. According to the Natural Resource Governance Institute (NRGI), Latin American and sub-Saharan African countries have borrowed at least $152 billion in loans from China backed by oil, minerals and metals since 2004, easy money that has contributed to higher debt levels. If we include loans from other countries such as Russia and other commodity importers, the total comes to $164 billion. Two state-owned Chinese banks, the China Development Bank and the Export-Import Bank, alone account for 77% of the loans. However, these arrangements have lost relevance following the collapse of international commodity prices in 2014, and numerous problems have emerged with existing agreements.

In recent years, some analysts have raised alarms about emerging market debt levels, which have more than doubled to $72 trillion in the last decade, while the IMF says the number of countries in trouble or at risk of debt has steadily increased. According to the NRGI, these loans have gone to developing countries that have limited access to global capital markets, and for this reason have been undermined by weak governance and opaque conditions, given also the low level of competition among lenders.

The details of how asset-backed lending works vary from case to case. In some circumstances, countries have ensured effective legal ownership of assets. In particular, this is what Zimbabwe has done with platinum deposits and even with the land under which the Chinese aqueduct runs. However, it is much more common to secure loans with revenues from commodity production. This is usually done through two parallel agreements: a loan agreement sets out the terms of the financing, including the collateralisation of the commodity revenues, which are often deposited in an escrow account designated for repayment of the loan; a purchase agreement then commits a Chinese company to purchase a certain number of commodities, thereby securing a revenue stream for the borrower. The value of the purchase agreement often exceeds the value of the loan by a significant margin, meaning that a small portion of the revenues from commodity exports is committed to repay the loan, while the borrowing country has full discretion over what to do with the rest.

Historically, oil has been the most popular option for collateralisation by far: around 82% of resource-backed loans from 2002 to 2014, when both commodity prices and resource-backed loan outflows fell sharply, were guaranteed by oil. This figure rises to 88% if loans to Turkmenistan guaranteed by natural gas are included. Another 8% went to metals such as copper, cobalt and platinum; the rest to a range of products from Ghanaian cocoa to Ukrainian wheat, and even to the generalised collateralisation of all export revenues to China, as is the case in Ethiopia and Uruguay.

Asset-backed loans simultaneously address China's interests in securing overseas business for its construction companies, access to raw material imports, and protection against the risk of non-repayment. As a global factory, China imports large quantities of raw materials and re-exports them as manufactured goods. In industrial sectors, the terms of the loans ensure that at least half of the value of a project, and typically much more, goes to Chinese companies. In sectors such as rail, road and power generation, Chinese companies were very successful in the 2000s and 2010s building the country's domestic infrastructure; but then they became victims of their own achievements as China's infrastructure improved dramatically and opportunities for new projects declined. However, these companies are important to the Chinese economy because they employ many people, and the government is reluctant to allow them to downsize significantly. That is why state-owned banks help them find business abroad, an otherwise difficult task in the context of a slowing global economy.

The implications for resource supply security are even more obvious. As of 2017, China is the world's largest importer of crude oil (16.7% of world trade), copper ore (43.2%), cobalt (43.7%) and grains (5.5%); and the third largest importer of natural gas (9.7%). All of these materials have been used to repay Chinese loans, which end up improving China's security by guaranteeing it access to raw materials directly at the production site. This mechanism also gives the country's enterprises the opportunity to upgrade their technological and managerial know-how to the level of large multinationals, to expand their production globally and to keep prices low.

Resource-backed loans also provide a degree of protection against political risk. The fact that they are "tied" to the presence of Chinese contractors means that banks can disburse funds directly to these contractors without going through high-risk local bank accounts; but it also means that host governments cannot unilaterally expel contractors without jeopardising access to financing. Repayment in commodities also means that China does not have to rely on governments remaining solvent to repay their loans. Officials at the China Development Bank, for example, were surprisingly forthright in their belief that repayment in Venezuelan oil would protect them from the fate of most of the others who had lent to the country's government.

Given these advantages, it is fair to ask why China does not use resource collateralisation even more often. In reality, this practice has several disadvantages. First, this method is usually only accepted by governments with few other sources of capital. In addition, resource-backed lending is generally not accompanied by measures to protect the transport of raw materials to the domestic market: most of China's imports arrive by sea and remain vulnerable to transport blockages, regardless of any agreement on debt relief. There are, admittedly, notable exceptions for loans secured by oil and gas that must be repaid through land pipelines from Russia and Turkmenistan respectively. However, both history and recent events indicate that a more likely (though less dramatic) threat to China's resource security lies not in blockades of oil tankers on the high seas, but in price shocks from events in producing regions, especially the Persian Gulf.

This is partly because many Middle Eastern producers have pre-existing relationships with the world's oil majors and do not feel the need to mortgage the nerve centres of their economies, but also because China feels overly dependent on the region and wants to diversify. Indeed, resource-backed loans tend to go disproportionately to distant regions: from 2002 to 2014, 43.5% went to Latin America, 32.2% to Eastern Europe and Central Asia, and 24.3% to Africa. This is rather surprising since one would expect China to focus on places where it can source minerals more cheaply. Consistent with the economics of transport costs, much African and Eurasian production is exported to China; most Latin American raw materials are not. In Ecuador, for example, a series of resource-backed loans and purchase orders led PetroChina and Sinopec to control between 80% and 90% of the country's oil production as of 2013, but at no point did more than 7% of Ecuadorian crude exports go to China. Hypothetically, the Beijing government could ask companies to redirect some raw materials to Chinese ports, but this is at best an insurance measure against a price shock that has not yet taken place. In normal times, as mentioned above, resource-guaranteed loans produce their positive effects in other ways: by supporting Chinese companies which can gain global experience, capacity and technical know-how and global market share through these contacts, and by keeping prices low through supply expansion.

This brings us to the other major limitation of resource-backed loans: they are only designed for certain countries. Using state funds to expand global commodity supply only makes sense in markets where others are unwilling to invest. Resource-backed loans tend to go to countries that are isolated from international capital markets and may not be able to reach their full commodity production capacity. Venezuela, the main beneficiary of resource-backed loans, has scared away most international investors with a series of nationalisations and a pledge to withdraw from the IMF and the World Bank. Russia's endemic corruption has made some investors cautious about entering the country, even before the invasion of Ukraine and Western sanctions. In third place was Angola, which began to fully exploit its oil reserves after the end of a civil war: at that point China (like many others) used oil as collateral to secure its loans in an uncertain environment.

In low-risk countries with better market reputations, this degree of risk management was neither necessary for Chinese companies nor acceptable to host governments who could find others willing to invest in their commodities without mortgaging mineral deposits or imposing restrictions on their choice of infrastructure contractors. The beneficiaries of resource-backed loans are therefore mainly countries where corruption is greatest.

Many borrowers have found it difficult to repay loans since the sharp fall in commodity prices in 2014 when crude oil prices were slashed in half, for example. Most transactions have been indexed to market prices, which means that debtors now have to generate more resources to keep up with payments. Currency markets can exacerbate this problem: most international trade and debt agreements are denominated in globally used "hard" currencies, such as the dollar and the euro, and falling export prices mean less currency coming in and therefore fewer resources to service the debt. Not all countries have had difficulties – Russia, for example, recently repaid an oil-financed loan ahead of schedule – but market trends have not been on the side of borrowers. Nor does this situation help China, which has reason to wonder how much of its money it will get back and whether the deals can benefit from guaranteed resources as hoped. The situation in Venezuela has been called a "creditor trap" in which systematic miscalculation of market price risk on both sides has led the China Development Bank to face losses of tens of billions and PetroChina to wonder how much oil it will actually be able to sell.

The Venezuelan case is indicative of a second problem: the collateralisation of resources has not provided the protection against embezzlement and misconduct that Beijing would have hoped. This has not been a problem in all countries, but where it has emerged, it has been far less manageable than market prices. A kleptocratic and inefficient system in Venezuela led to billions being wasted, meaning that Petroléos de Venezuela (PDVSA), the state oil company, did not have enough money in the bank to maintain production: one of the worst economic collapses in memory ensued. Less dramatic versions of this story have followed elsewhere. In Ecuador, for example, a former administration is under investigation for the disappearance of billions in oil-related infrastructure funds. The tying of loan contracts to select Chinese companies has opened the door to several types of malfeasance. First, the opacity surrounding these non-competitive, closed-door deals makes it fairly easy for Chinese contractors to subcontract to local firms with limited oversight, providing an alternative route to corruption in the absence of loans directly to government bank accounts. Corruption and general mismanagement can jeopardise economic output and thus the repayment of loans. Thus, even where local corruption is not a problem, the lack of competition in the bidding process results in a limited incentive to do high quality work. Of six Chinese hydroelectric dams built in Ecuador, for example, none were completed on time, and many had serious quality problems, including several thousand cracks and structural defects in a billion-dollar colossus in Coca Codo. And in many cases, low-quality work does not generate sufficient economic return to repay the borrower.

Asset-backed lending began to play a smaller role in Chinese policy after commodity prices collapsed in 2014. Some debtor governments have openly spoken out against those asset-backed loans, especially where the new leadership has begun to question the relationships of its predecessors with China, and most of the major borrowers of the commodity boom era are now making much less use of resource collateralisation. An early sign of trouble came from Ghana, where in 2015 the government decided not to withdraw the second half of a planned $3 billion oil-backed loan amid concerns about low prices. Much more has happened since then. Angola's new president has pledged to stop borrowing with oil as collateral. The IMF included debt restructuring to China in its rescue package for the Republic of Congo, and in Ecuador China's continued involvement has been limited to a small loan not backed by oil. In Venezuela, China turned to "defensive lending" to boost local crude production, for the sole purpose of servicing existing debt.

Many of these loans have financed necessary infrastructure, such as roads and dams, but in many cases have led to crippling levels of debt for recipient countries, which risk losing collateral that was worth more than the value of the loan itself. The collapse in oil prices in 2014, for example, hit the Republic of Congo and Chad hard, as they were unable to offer cargoes of crude oil as debt repayment. To qualify for the IMF bailout programme, Chad had to restructure its oil-backed loan with Glencore (Anglo-Swiss international commodities trading giant) with the help of banks, which it managed to do in 2018. Congo was also granted a conditional bailout worth $2 billion from the IMF and other lenders, but these payments have been frozen since the government's negotiations with Glencore and Trafigura stalled (the latter is another Swiss commodities trading company).

In Ghana, the IMF has warned that a planned increase in bauxite production to meet repayments on a $2 billion loan from China's state-owned company Sinohydro may not be possible. Guinea has signed a $20 billion loan worth 200% of its GDP, which is also backed by bauxite production (a significant part of this loan, according to NRGI, has not yet been used). Although bauxite production began in Guinea when concessions were made to the Chinese as part of the agreement, there is still little public information on how repayments will be made.

In conclusion, China's lending against guarantees of resource supplies combines a country with a strong construction sector and a shortage of raw materials (China) with partners in the opposite situation. The basic idea is not wrong, but the implementation problems are numerous. Scorched by events in Venezuela in particular, China is likely to be more cautious in the future, as are many debtors. This change should not be the result of an isolated decision, but rather part of a broader trend towards moderation, as previous agreements have caused China to lose money and its foreign exchange reserves no longer seem bottomless. In addition to quantitative tightening, there could be qualitative changes in the structure of future resource-financed operations.

Towards a "renminbi bloc"?

Informally, the renminbi has long been accepted as a settlement currency in cross-border trade with neighbouring countries such as Laos, Mongolia, Myanmar, Nepal, North Korea and Vietnam, resulting in a substantial growth in the volume of renminbi notes circulating beyond China's borders. While overall estimates vary widely and reliability is questionable, it is clear that the numbers are no longer trivial.

In Mongolia, according to the *Economist*, up to 60% of the cash in circulation today could be renminbi. The formal authorisation of business establishment in renminbi, which began with a limited pilot scheme in 2009, was extended to all Chinese enterprises by early 2012. In addition, since September 2010, foreign companies have been allowed to open cross-border renminbi settlement accounts with locally registered banks in China, further expanding opportunities for using the renminbi on a regular basis. And along the way, the PBoC has been busy building a new Chinese international payment system, a vital technical infrastructure to facilitate cross-border billing and payments.

Agreements to introduce direct trade between the renminbi and local currencies have been negotiated in several foreign financial centres, including London, Paris, Frankfurt, Luxembourg, Singapore and Taiwan. In each location, a single clearing bank has been designated for renminbi-denominated transactions. The results of all these initiatives have been impressive: by the end of 2014, around 20% of Chinese trade had been settled in renminbi, compared to five years earlier, when this share was essentially zero.

As for another key ingredient of any currency that aspires to play an international role – the trust of those who use it – the Chinese government's idea seems to be to reshape identity and interests through the rise of "political China." Here too, Chinese soft power is proving highly effective. The internationalisation of the renminbi can spread because market players are convinced of its legitimacy, confirming the Middle Kingdom's renewed prominence in the community of nations. To paraphrase Robert Mundell, foreigners may come to believe that China, as an emerging great power, should have a great currency, and therefore gain unconditional confidence in its currency in the belief that sooner or later it will become a global currency. Both lines of reasoning make sense.

The gravitational pull of the Chinese economy is undeniable. And in fact the internationalisation of the renminbi is hard to imagine without it. But is the economic dimension alone enough to make the renminbi competitive? In this respect, a large dose of scepticism is justified. The reason lies in the multiple roles of an international currency and the considerable differences between them. The economic dimension is clearly the key to the role of money as a means of commercial invoicing and payment. In this regard, it is not surprising that the renminbi has already begun to establish itself as a trade currency; and this role, in turn, seems to be encouraging the use of the renminbi also as an anchor currency, in a way reminiscent of the experience of the German mark in the 1970s and 1980s. Experts debate how far the process has progressed, with some sources expressing much scepticism. But a variety of studies seem to confirm that a growing number of East Asian countries now give greater weight to the renminbi in managing their exchange rates, forming what would be a nascent "renminbi bloc." These countries include major trading nations such as Indonesia, Malaysia, the Philippines, Singapore, South Korea, Taiwan and Thailand. Unofficially, the renminbi also circulates in Macau, Laos, Cambodia, North Korea, Myanmar, Mongolia, Nepal, Vietnam and Zimbabwe. In South-East Asia, a genuine renminbiisation is under way, the most interesting case being that of Indonesia.

***

According to a SWIFT report, 215 billion renminbi were circulating in Indonesia in 2017. Currently about 10% of Indonesia's global trade uses renminbi. In 2018, the value of renminbi clearing reached 201.2 billion, accounting for about 63% of the entire Indonesian market. Bank of China ranked first in Indonesia's market share by clearing value. The increasing internationalisation of the renminbi is facilitated, among other things, by expanding economic ties between Jakarta and Beijing. China is now Indonesia's largest trading partner, with twice as much trade as compared to the United States. Voluminous investment from China has also made its way into the archipelago, particularly with the implementation of the BRI.

Chinese companies in Indonesia have also started using the renminbi. China Life Insurance Indonesia (CLII), for example, has launched the first multi-purpose individual life insurance product in renminbi in the Indonesian market, known as the CLII Privilege Insurance Plan. CLII said the move was part of the strategy of its parent company, China Life Insurance Group, to support the renminbi's internationalisation process.

Some Chinese banks, such as Bank of China and Industrial and Commercial Bank of China (ICBC), have also opened branches in Indonesia. These banks help expand the use of the renminbi in the country through mechanisms such as renminbi deposits, renminbi remittances, and domestic and cross-border renminbi fund transfers. The same banks also offer various banking products and services to corporations, small and medium-sized enterprises and individuals through branches located in Indonesia. In addition, they have collaborated with local banks to help internationalise the renminbi in the country. ICBC for example has collaborated with Bank Mandiri to provide banking products and services related to renminbi transactions. As a result of this collaboration, at the beginning of 2018, renminbi transactions facilitated by Bank Mandiri Group totalled approximately 507 items worth 601 million renminbi.

The expansion of renminbi usage in Indonesia cannot be understood without taking into account the bilateral currency swap agreement signed by Bank Indonesia and PBoC in 2018. The agreement was worth 200 billion renminbi ($30 billion at the time, doubling the previous threshold of 100 billion renminbi). The purpose was to allow trade transactions using the currencies of both countries, which can shorten and simplify such transactions compared to using international trade currencies or hard currencies such as the dollar (in which case each country must first convert its currencies into dollars). Bank Indonesia had previously signed similar agreements with Japan and the European Union.

Although renminbi bonds in Indonesia remain limited (less than 1%), the increasing use of this currency in trade transactions with China is likely to lead Jakarta to issue renminbi-denominated sovereign debt. In fact, the Indonesian Ministry of Finance has admitted that it is currently studying the possibility of issuing a renminbi-denominated panda bond that will thus augment Indonesia's foreign currency bonds, which have so far only been issued in dollars, euros and Japanese yen. (Other countries that have used panda bonds as a source of budget funding include the Philippines and Poland.)

The use of the renminbi in Indonesia is set to grow in the coming years, thanks to the continued implementation of the BRI and the PBoC's recent introduction of electronic payment in e-RMB, which will facilitate online transactions. Another powerful driver is the Covid-19 pandemic. More importantly, Indonesia is convinced of the desirability of using the renminbi, due to a number of advantages. One is that the renminbi is more stable than the dollar, which fluctuates easily against the currencies of other countries. Thus, in terms of transaction costs, the Chinese currency is cheaper and safer, and can reduce exchange rate risk. Another reason why the use of the Chinese currency is likely to proliferate in Indonesia is that Jakarta sees China as one of the most financially sound countries in the world. Indonesia, needing foreign capital, will certainly want to take advantage of these opportunities by opening the door to the renminbi. President Joko "Jokowi" Widodo has even floated the idea of making the renminbi a reference currency.

The rising flow of capital from China should not, however, cause Indonesia to allow Beijing to dictate terms. Rather, China should continue to follow the rules of the game set by Indonesia, to ensure that wider use of the renminbi benefits both sides. Indonesia, for its part, needs to encourage its key players to open up to the use of the renminbi when they do business. The most crucial obstacle to the wider use of the renminbi comes from those economic operators who still do not trust the renminbi in commercial transactions. A change in the mindset of business people in both countries is therefore crucial for the future of the renminbi.

The expansion of the renminbi in Europe

Europe is at the forefront of China's efforts to raise the renminbi to international status. China has built up a major trading infrastructure in the Old World, making it the largest renminbi market outside Hong Kong. Europe is an important trading partner for China, and vice versa: in 2018, China imported goods from Europe worth over $2 trillion, around 18% of its total imports. In this sense, the opening of the European market to the renminbi will progressively make it easier for Chinese companies to make direct payments in their own currency for European goods and services that they wish to import.

For their part, European countries have competed to attract renminbi clearing activities; as a result the necessary trading infrastructure is largely in place. China's internationalisation project has thus gained ground in Europe as players here have been receptive to working with Chinese partners to create a supporting infrastructure. They believe that they can gain commercial benefits in the form of easier access to the Chinese market, greater visibility and thus export opportunities to China. (In this regard, we should consider that Chinese companies have limited access to foreign currency, so the possibility of making overseas purchases in renminbi could lead to a surge in imports of European goods and services.)

In more detail, it should be noted that the strengths of the UK – the largest currency market in the world, with a business-friendly legal system to boot – are difficult to replicate elsewhere, and indeed London is likely to remain the main renminbi clearing house in Europe. However, Paris, Frankfurt and Luxembourg have also all carved out a significant role for themselves in the renminbi market. Overall, in any case, international use of the currency remains far below its potential, mainly due to China's self-imposed restrictions on convertibility. Brexit also could temporarily damage the UK's renminbi business, and in fact Britain has been making plans to avoid losing its position for some time, as we will see more below.

Europe accounted for 9.4% of renminbi transactions around the world in 2018 (after Hong Kong with 76.2% of the global total). If Hong Kong renminbi liquidity is excluded, the European share of the total rises to 40.1%, with the bulk (24.7%) in the United Kingdom. France was second with 6.3%, followed by Germany with 3.3% and Luxembourg with 1.9%.

China is also having some success in promoting the use of the renminbi in Europe through its cross-border interbank payment system (CIPS). Beijing introduced CIPS in October 2015 as an alternative to the American SWIFT, which currently takes the lion's share of international payments. In 2018, CIPS handled payments worth around 26 trillion renminbi, a boom of more than 80% compared to 2017. As of 2019, there are more than 100 banks worldwide using CIPS: 30 in Japan, 23 in Russia, 19 in Taiwan, 16 in Singapore, 15 in the UK. The initial success of CIPS was largely driven by its use in BRI-member countries, suggesting that Xi's flagship foreign policy programme is already contributing to the internationalisation of the renminbi. It should not be forgotten, however, that even in 2017 there were still more than fifty economies in the BRI supporter group where the percentage of renminbi use in cross-border transactions was less than 5%. Moverover, much stronger economic ties between China and the BRI countries would be needed to propel the renminbi to the point of becoming a currency used in many of these economies. On the other hand, official documents for European renminbi internationalisation projects cite the very reason for implementing the BRI: Chinese companies and their partners need to finance and pay for the construction of vast networks of ports, roads and railways. Therefore, it would be easier for them if their respective European partners accepted payments in renminbi, instead having to buy dollars first as they do now.

The advance of the renminbi in Europe has also been facilitated by the willingness of major European countries to foster the development of a market that advances the commercial interests of their companies. On the one hand, European governments and institutions have good reason to be receptive to renminbi internationalisation initiatives, given that their economies are much more dependent on exports than the United States. In 2018, goods trade accounted for 71.2% of German GDP, 45.2% of French GDP and 41% of British GDP, while it was only 20.8% of US GDP. On the other hand, a larger European market also presents significant risks: European companies trading in renminbi could easily find themselves at the mercy of currency movements entirely decided in Beijing. This may not be desirable, as Europe sees China more and more as a strategic competitor. Compared to Pacific powers such as the US and Japan, however, European governments have been less concerned about the potential risks of cooperating with China and tend to focus more on the trade benefits.

According to an article by the German research centre Merics, European regulators and financial institutions have adopted a very pragmatic attitude towards the needs of businesses when choosing how to promote the growth of the European renminbi market. Sherry Madera, until recently special advisor to the City of London Corporation on Asia, stressed the importance of London's growing ties with China in the future. Hubertus Vaeth of Frankfurt Main Finance and former head of Asian research at Deutsche Bank, took a similar stance, saying Frankfurt has a unique opportunity to witness the emergence of a new global currency. Even more pragmatically, the French consul general in Hong Kong, Arnaud Barthelemy, pointed out that French companies want to regulate trade in renminbi so they can offer French banks renminbi-denominated bonds and funds.

Good European receptivity has encouraged China to be particularly active in creating initiatives to promote the circulation of its currency. Renminbi clearing banks have been set up and memoranda of understanding have been signed for the development of financial infrastructure. European financial organisations have been given access to Chinese financial products through the RQFII programme, and Chinese banks have established themselves in Europe. These are the ingredients for the creation of real hubs to facilitate renminbi transactions, namely the appointment of an official settlement bank for offshore renminbi transactions, a quota of renminbi Qualified Foreign Institutional Investors for reinvestment in China, and a swap facility to support renminbi settlement. The network of offshore centres provides a framework to expedite offshore transactions, complementing onshore market reforms and international successes such as the inclusion of the renminbi in the IMF's SDR basket.

The two European central banks responsible for most of the European markets where the renminbi is traded, namely the European Central Bank (ECB) and the Bank of England (BoE), have both signed currency swap agreements with China and help promote renminbi lending by ensuring a basic level of liquidity in the market. Speaking in 2019, former BoE governor Sir Mervyn King described the swap agreements as one of the most important steps in promoting renminbi business in London.

Each of the European countries hosting a financial centre that has also started trading in renminbi is strong in a particular segment of the market. London is the leader in foreign exchange, Germany in trade, but for investments and deposits Luxembourg is the main marketplace.

European countries' efforts to build markets in renminbi have not been identical: some have scaled up the amount of trade in renminbi-invoiced goods, while others have focused on developing renminbi-denominated financial products. That said, all the major European countries that trade in renminbi are to some extent active in all these channels.

The UK handles most renminbi payments and foreign exchange transactions. It has a large trade deficit with China and exports less than France or Germany in absolute terms. In 2018, it exported $23.8 billion worth of goods to China, but had a trade deficit of $33.4 billion. With the help of a business-friendly legal system, the UK's large financial and currency markets thus compensate for the lower amount of trade. In 2014, the UK exported £20 billion in financial services to the EU. European financial markets are open (although the post-Brexit scenario could change this significantly), companies earning renminbi in other countries can deposit or trade them in London, and the UK financial system then allocates them elsewhere. This network-effect makes London an attractive deposit destination for companies from across Europe. But while the effects of the Brexit on London's future role in the internationalisation of the renminbi are still difficult to assess, China's suspension in January 2020 of the new London-Shanghai Stock Connect has shown how politicised the space for financial cooperation with Beijing still is. According to sources quoted in the media, tensions over Britain's stance on Hong Kong protests led China to temporarily halt the Stock Connect scheme, which was only launched in 2019 with the aim of attracting more renminbi business to the UK. The Stock Connect in fact enables equity traders in both cities mutual access to the market through depository receipts, which allows London-based financial institutions to buy renminbi-denominated shares listed in China. The link also aims to give Chinese companies the opportunity to list newly issued shares denominated in pounds and dollars directly on the London Stock Exchange, thus helping them to self-finance in foreign currency.

Germany initially hoped to make Frankfurt the main European clearing house for financial activities related to trade with China. This objective seems sensible as trade in goods dominates Germany's economic relations with China, much more so than for the UK or France, but intention has not yet materialised. According to the monthly renminbi tracker managed by SWIFT, the world's largest payment system provider, only a small proportion of Sino-German trade is denominated in Chinese currency, with most trade still in other currencies. Emblematic in this respect is the operation of CEINEX, a Sino-German joint venture that provides for the exchange of Chinese financial products between the Shanghai Stock Exchange and Deutsche Börse. From its Frankfurt office, CEINEX allows Chinese companies to list "D-shares," i.e. shares denominated in euros and renminbi that are sold on the Frankfurt Stock Exchange. However, only Shanghai-listed companies with A-shares can list on the Frankfurt Stock Exchange and so far, most deals have been conducted in euros. (In 2018 only 3.5% of transactions were in renminbi.) The most notable company to list shares through CEINEX was white goods manufacturer Qingdao Haier.

France has the second largest share of renminbi in European markets, with a strategy that lies somewhere between that of Germany and the UK. Much of France's trade with China is conducted in renminbi. (More than 55% of payments between France and China/Hong Kong were settled in renminbi in 2017, according to the SWIFT tracker.) But France's currency market is smaller than the UK's: in 2016, it handled around 2.7% of global forex transactions and around 6% of currency transactions involving renminbi.

Luxembourg focuses on deposits, loans and bonds and has the largest European pool of renminbi deposits, loans and bonds. This country has competed for the most extensive market share in renminbi, allowing Chinese banks to set up branches that ship from abroad in their own currency. Compensating for the Grand Duchy's small size is Luxembourg's position in the Eurozone and its ability to offer the European banking passport (which allows banks domiciled in that country to do business in all European Economic Area member states). The strategy proved successful: China's major state banks (with the exception of the Bank of China) established their European headquarters in Luxembourg.

Despite London's dominance, efforts to build renminbi markets in continental Europe will continue. Joachim Nagel, who served on the executive board of the Deutsche Bundesbank from 2010 to 2016, said that euro clearing for renminbi assets should be located in a country that is part of the Eurosystem. However, it will be difficult for continental European countries to oust the UK as the leading renminbi market without restricting capital flows. Indeed, the UK enjoys advantages that other countries cannot easily compete with: a business-friendly legal system; the world's largest currency market; a historic connection with

Hong Kong (where British banks are present); an English-speaking environment making it easier for Chinese companies to work there; and – and perhaps most importantly – the size and connectivity of its financial markets. Since continental European players cannot simply replicate these competitive factors, mounting a determined challenge to London would involve taking self-defeating measures, such as restricting their companies' access to British markets. But it is very unlikely that capital controls would be imposed, as this would be a violation of property rights that democratic countries hardly ever resort to. Any restriction on the flow of capital between the European continent and the UK would effectively limit EU savers and investors from accessing the returns offered there. (Two democratic countries that have resorted to such exceptional and temporary measures were Argentina in 2019 and Greece in 2015.) And without capital controls, the renminbi can still be freely deposited in the UK.

Brexit may take some financial business away from the UK, but it is unlikely that the UK will be marginalised from financial markets. If upon leaving the EU, the UK also leaves the European Economic Area – which seems likely – it will lose its European banking passporting rights that allow UK-based banks to sell financial services directly and actively to EU-based customers. The UK would then have to apply for separate licences in each member country and find intermediaries to work with. But even without a banking passport, EU-based companies would still be able to buy interest-bearing products directly from UK banks. European companies obtaining renminbi from foreign trade would therefore still be able to deposit these sums in London.

At the end of July 2020, Italy also joined the small and select group of EU member states (Poland, Portugal and Hungary, with the possible addition of Austria) authorised to issue panda bonds on the Chinese interbank market. The issue of three-year panda bonds amounted to a total value of 1 billion renminbi (€130 million) with a fixed yield of 4.5%. This is the concrete outcome of one of the agreements signed between Italy and China during President Xi's visit to Rome in March 2019, during which a Memorandum of Understanding was signed between the two countries (as with the other EU Member States) for cooperation in the implementation of the BRI.

***

As mentioned in Chapter 1, a panda bond is a renminbi-denominated instrument floated by an issuer based outside the PRC (or by a Chinese company with registered offices abroad). The term derives from the practice of naming local currency bonds by foreign issuers after the mascot of the country in question (hence Australia has kangaroo bonds). Usually financial institutions handle bond issues, as was the case for the first two panda bonds issued in October 2005, on the same day, by the International Finance Corporation and the Asian Development Bank, for a total value of 4 billion renminbi. The Italian issue, by Cassa Depositi e Prestiti, followed the Portuguese issue of May 2020 (for 2 billion renminbi, equal to 250 million euro) and the Polish issue of June 2016, the first by a European country.

The real expansion of these instruments began in 2015, when HSBC obtained approval to issue commercial panda bonds, and sovereign and quasi-sovereign issues by Korea and the Canadian province of British Columbia also began. While financial institutions and governments clearly dominate the pool of issuers, the first corporate issuance by Germany's Daimler was approved in 2014 for 500 million renminbi, followed by many others including one in 2019 of 3.5 billion renminbi by BMW (according to Global Capital's Panda Bond Database). It appears that other big names among multinationals have applied to the NDRC, but without success.

To date, available data on the overall value of panda bonds are conflicting. According to Fitch, the total amount of panda bonds issued in the China Interbank Bond Market (CIBM) had reached 123.4 billion renminbi by the end of 2017; Dealogic data show, panda bonds worth around 30 billion renminbi were issued between 2005 and 2016; and referencing the World Bank's International Finance Corporation, the panda bond market exceeded 320 billion renminbi by 2020. Although growing dramatically, the panda bond market, now worth about $48 billion, remains tiny compared to the size of China's entire $13 trillion bond market. Among the reasons are high issuing costs compared to the rest of the world and still limited interest from investors.

But what are the benefits and costs of issuing panda bonds these bonds represent for European issuers and their Chinese counterparts? Originally introduced as a financial instrument to increase investment opportunities in renminbi, panda bonds are now used by foreign companies as a platform to raise funds in countries where access to credit is almost impossible for foreign companies operating there. Therefore a way for issuing companies to raise otherwise inaccessible funds, albeit at a much higher cost than in Europe. The three-year panda bonds issued in May 2019 by Portugal pay a rate of 4.09%, while on the European market Portugal, despite having severe liquidity problems between 2011 and 2014, can at most borrow at a yield of less than 1%. The 4.5% rate on Italian issues today is much higher than the prevailing rate in Europe, even though CDP's rating is AAA.

Since the cost of issuance is higher than elsewhere, it is clear that panda bonds offer other benefits. As for corporate issuance, poor access to credit forces companies to find other financing channels. Sovereign or quasi-sovereign issuance, on the other hand, is motivated by a desire to please the Chinese authorities, supporting their goal of raising the international status of the renminbi and improving China's profile in international financial markets, by alternative means than a progressive and real opening of the domestic credit sector and capital account (which Beijing does not want, to avoid the danger of importing instability). At the same time, European issuers hope to obtain a fast track in Chinese investment flows into Europe.

In order to accelerate the growth of the market for these bonds, the chairman of the China Securities Regulatory Commission, Guo Shuqing, announced some time ago that he would allow them to be issued and listed on the stock exchange, whereas up to now panda bonds have been issued and circulated mainly on the interbank market. The expansion of the panda bond market would provide companies with an alternative to the other renminbi bonds currently available to foreign companies, the dim sum bonds issued in Hong Kong, which are only issued offshore and only placed with international investors. The prospect of a panda bond market competing with the dim sum bond market may be attractive to Beijing both from a strictly economic and financial point of view – many more companies and institutions would have an incentive to issue the former as the onshore market is much larger than the offshore one – and from a political perspective as well. A downsizing of Hong Kong's financial role (central to mainland China's growth and international integration strategy) would reduce Beijing's need to grant broad independence to what will remain a Special Administrative Region only until 2047.

Guo has always been a strong supporter of panda bonds since his time as president of the China Construction Bank, and as early as

2009 he suggested that the US government consider issuing renminbi bonds, rather than selling US Treasury debt to borrow money from China.

Today, the BRI is offering a vehicle generously permitting foreigners to borrow Chinese savings at a higher rate than in their home countries. It is also a way to further expand Chinese influence in Europe: as more and more securities are issued in China by European governments and companies, Europe's dependence on good relations with China grows.

China's lending abroad: sovereign on market terms

China's overseas lending has unique characteristics compared to that provided by other major economies after World War II. First, capital outflows from China are almost exclusively sovereign loans and thus controlled by the Chinese government. The main creditors are state-owned banks, plus a number of state-owned enterprises. Private banks play a minor role. Moreover, the terms and characteristics of Chinese state loans abroad seem in many respects more similar to commercial loans. Most are dollar-denominated and issued at interest rates that reflect a risk premium and with contractual features that resemble private bank loans. In low-income countries, China's loans are generally repayable at interest rates between 2 and 3%, in contrast to the interest-free loans and grants that highly-indebted poor countries typically receive from most other bilateral and multilateral creditors. Even in emerging markets and middle-income countries, most loans are granted on market terms, i.e. with interest rates comparable to those prevailing in the bond or private lending markets. In 2010, for example, Ecuador borrowed $1.7 billion from the China Export-Import Bank at 7% interest for a period of fifteen years. Similarly, over the last ten years, Angola has borrowed a total of $20 billion from Chinese state banks at an average interest rate of 6% and with maturities ranging from 12 to 17 years.

More importantly, Chinese loans abroad often enjoy a relatively high degree of seniority, as they are often backed by collateral: interest and principal repayments are often secured, either in the form of commodities (e.g. export earnings from raw materials and agricultural products), or by giving the creditor the right to a share in the profits of state-owned enterprises. No other official lender guarantees its international loans in this way, at least not systematically.

Institutionally and legally, Chinese loans also have features that make them more like commercial arrangements than institutional ones. Loans are granted by a variety of creditors, including more than a dozen public banks and state-owned enterprises acting as private entities. In addition, loan agreements often have the appearance of commercial loans, with secrecy and arbitration clauses, so that repayment amounts or any details of default or restructuring are kept out of the public domain. All these peculiarities are very unusual for government loans, such as those granted by OECD governments and Paris Club member countries since the war. About 70% of Paris Club credits to low-income and emerging countries are in fact granted in the form of official development assistance as defined by the OECD, i.e. they have a concessional character and a grant rate of at least 25%. The US government, for its part, usually provides funds for military and economic cooperation in the form of grants rather than loans. The same is true for official creditors in Europe, where the European Stability Mechanism (ESM) provides loans with maturities of up to 30 years and almost zero risk premiums. In summary, China's official loans abroad are not comparable to the lending activities of most other creditor governments: more than half of the loans were extended on commercial terms, only 15% on concessional terms, and no information is available on the remaining 35% of loans.

Moreover, most of China's foreign loans are denominated in foreign currency (85% in US dollars), while renminbi-denominated loans account for a very small share. Finally, estimates suggest that about 50% of Chinese overseas loans are secured by a wide range of commodities, as we will see below.

Two banks have so far dominated China's foreign lending universe: the Chinese Export-Import Bank and the China Development Bank, both owned by China's State Council. Together, they account for over 75% of all direct cross-border lending between 2000 and 2017, while government agencies such as the Ministry of Commerce play only a minor role. It is therefore clear that the lack of transparency on much of China's overseas lending activities could be overcome simply by publishing the balance sheet and credit data of these two banks to sovereign states.

Towards a new debt crisis with Chinese characteristics?

One of the main challenges in exploring the large-scale official lending boom in China is its opacity. The Chinese government does not release data on its own foreign lending. Moreover, China is not a member of the most important creditor organisations that provide data on official lending and restructuring, notably the Paris Club of creditor governments but also the OECD. Data from the creditor side are therefore not available.

Also from the debtor side the coverage of Chinese loan data is very incomplete. As extensively reported by Horn and colleagues (2019), one reason is the way the Chinese government lends abroad. Loans are rarely borrowed bilaterally, i.e. from government to government. Rather, almost all Chinese overseas lending is done through Chinese state-owned entities, and the recipients tend to be state-owned enterprises. Statistical offices in developing countries do not often collect this type of loans, so that international debt statistics suffer from chronic underreporting. According to the IMF (2018 data), fewer than one in ten low-income countries report non-government public enterprise debt. As a result, debtor countries themselves have an incomplete picture of how much they have borrowed from China and on what terms.

Understandably, not even the private financial industry monitors China's state-led cross-border borrowing flows. Rating agencies such as S&P or Moody's track debt and credit (default) events on private-to-private flows. For similar reasons, major data providers such as Bloomberg or Dealogic failed to identify the international boom in Chinese loans. They closely follow publicly-traded debt instruments, such as sovereign bonds or private syndicated loans, but Chinese sovereign loans, which are not priced in international markets, are missing from their analyses.

The data provided by the central bank statistics of the countries involved in the BRI are not helpful either. China started reporting to the BIS in 2015, but the government has not agreed to make data on bilateral claims public (country by country). Only aggregate data on Chinese claims are available, and only up to 2015. In any case, these data indicate that China only reports part of its overseas claims to the BIS, with large reporting gaps, particularly in high-risk countries.

According to Horn and colleagues (2019), one potential explanation for the incomplete reporting to the BIS is China's "circular" lending strategy that minimises the risk of default on its foreign loans. More specifically, for risky borrowers, China's state-owned banks often choose not to transfer money to accounts controlled by the recipient government. Instead, the loans are disbursed directly to the Chinese contractor carrying out the construction project abroad: the loans thus remain within the Chinese financial system, making it more difficult for recipient countries to misuse the money. Since this type of overseas lending is not actually transferred across borders, there is nothing to report to the BIS, which may explain part of China's wide reporting gap.

This lack of knowledge about the amount of China's foreign loans is a major problem for both debt management, surveillance work and asset pricing. Analysing debt sustainability becomes difficult if a large part of a country's debt and debt service is excluded from official aggregates. The same applies to the IMF's surveillance work. Similarly, pricing government bonds and assessing risk becomes difficult when a large share of a country's external debt is unknown. Finally, in the event of a default, opacity on the stock and composition of a country's debt prevents an orderly process to manage and exit the crisis.

Results from recent research (Horn at al., 2019) show that about 50% of China's loans are "hidden." Neither the IMF nor the World Bank nor the credit rating agencies report on these hidden debt securities, which have grown to over $200 billion as of 2016. The problem of China's hidden loans is particularly acute in crisis countries such as Venezuela, Zimbabwe and Iran. Indeed, China does not report any bank credit to the BIS vis-à-vis these countries, despite sizeable known loan flows over the past fifteen years. These findings have important implications for debt sustainability in recipient countries, not least because Chinese government lendings abroad differ markedly from other official lenders such as the World Bank or OECD governments.

Regarding the hidden stocks of Chinese debt owed by developing countries, for the top fifty recipient countries, the stock of debt owed to China rose to an average of 17% of GDP in 2016. Of this debt, 40%, or around 7% of GDP, is not reported in the official statistics of debtor countries.

There is also great heterogeneity among hidden debts owed to China. About half of the sample does not show high levels of hidden debt. However, for about 25 countries hidden debts to China exceed 5% of GDP and 12 of them owe more than 10% of their GDP.

***

In their two-hundred-year history of capital flows, Carmen Reinhart and Richard Trebesch show how the global economy has faced, since 2012, both a collapse in commodity prices and a sharp decline in capital inflows (and in some cases outflows). However, in contrast to previous cases of similar adverse shocks over the long period these researchers studied, the global incidence of sovereign defaults ticked up only modestly.

Sovereign debt restructurings involving Chinese loans have nonetheless increased, since 2000, to at least 140 external debt restructurings and debt cancellations with governments and public entities in developing and emerging countries.

China's overseas lending boom has important implications for financial stability and debt sustainability in recipient countries. Moreover, the ongoing Chinese lending boom must be compared with historical experiences. In particular, it is useful to draw a parallel with the syndicated lending boom of the 1970s, in which poor and resource-rich countries in Africa, Asia and Latin America received large amounts of foreign capital from Western banks. Those massive capital inflows were responsible for a wave of financial crises and economic depression in the early 1980s.

Once China's hidden loans are accounted for, many countries show a different debt dynamics. These countries include mostly Asian countries near to China and resource-rich African countries.

Many of the recipients are low-income countries that not so long ago defaulted in the wake of the aforementioned 1980s crisis. Indeed, many of China's heavy borrowers had already benefited from the HIPC and MDRI (Multilateral Debt Relief Initiative) debt relief initiatives of the 2000s and are reaching again high debt levels.

The picture becomes even more worrying when considering that Chinese loans are not on concessional terms, but on market terms and usually have shorter maturities.

Developing and emerging countries are now much more indebted to China than to all other major creditor governments combined. Indeed, according to some recent estimates, developing and emerging countries owe $380 billion to China, compared to $246 billion in debt for the group of 22 Paris Club member countries.

The group of countries most exposed to China are Low Income Developing Countries (LIDCs). Many are commodity exporters and some are also former Highly Indebted Poor Countries (HIPCs) that benefited from large-scale official debt relief in the 1990s and 2000s. In 2017, the average indebtedness of HIPCs to China was 11% of GDP. In comparison, emerging market countries incurred debt to China amounting to 6.5% of their GDP. Another highly exposed group are the oil-exporting countries, such as Angola, Ecuador, Niger and Venezuela, for which the average debt is 8.8% of GDP (while the median is 3.6%). This reflects the fact that some BRI countries have already borrowed heavily from China (raising the average), while others have only recently joined the BRI and are not as seriously indebted. This is the case of Eastern European and Middle Eastern countries.

The regions most heavily indebted to China are the Far East and Central Asia, including small, highly exposed economies in close geographical proximity to China, such as Laos, Cambodia and the Kyrgyz Republic. Sub-Saharan Africa and Latin America follow, as well as parts of the MENA region. Debt flows to Eastern Europe are smaller when measured as a share of the debtor country's GDP, but credit amounts to Europe have grown substantially over the past five years.

BRI project financing has contributed a great deal to this scenario, which can, in some circumstances, magnify the indebtedness of recipient countries to an alarming degree. However, increased exposure to China does not necessarily translate into a risk of debt unsustainability. The pre-existing stock of accumulated debt and the number of countries to which debt is contracted are two key variables.

Among the BRI partners that are most indebted to China, three groups can be distinguished. The first is made up of countries that already had a high external debt to GDP ratio and, by receiving considerable amounts of funding from Beijing, have worsened their debt position; these countries are now at risk of a debt crisis. The second group of countries, on the other hand, has a lower external debt-to-GDP ratio, but has incurred hefty debts to China (Afghanistan and Cambodia), thus risking becoming financially dependent on Beijing, as being indebted to a single large creditor is riskier than having more fragmented debt among creditor countries. Finally, a third group has a high external debt-to-GDP ratio but little Chinese financing (e.g. Egypt); the debt crisis these countries face is not only due to the Chinese financing they receive, but to the pre-existing conditions of their external debt-to-GDP ratio.

By 2020, some countries had already defaulted or were obliged to introduce debt restructuring programmes (Argentina, Belize, Ecuador, Lebanon, Suriname, Zambia). In comparison, in the great financial crisis of 2008-09, there were only three sovereign defaults, which means that many poor and indebted countries are now in more serious condition. In particular, the events in Zambia in the autumn of 2020 risk becoming the prototype for the next debt crisis in many developing countries. Indeed, Zambia, an African copper producer, was already in bad shape when the coronavirus pandemic broke out, having borrowed $12 billion from international creditors. In addition, this country has borrowed more than $3 billion from Chinese banks, such as the China Export-Import Bank and the China Development Bank, according to Standard & Poor's. But the opacity of these debts and disagreements over how to deal with them has made handling the crisis very complicated. Bondholders do not want to accept reductions in the yields on their investments, while Chinese creditors do not want debt relief. However, the IMF cannot accept a Zambian economic rescue programme without making sure that its debts are sustainable. The impasse led to a default on bond payments at the end of October 2020, and the country found itself in financial limbo.

Over the next five years, the expected probability of sovereign default is very high (between 30% and 55%) for a large group of countries, including, in descending order, Argentina, Angola, Pakistan, Iraq, Kenya, Ghana, Bolivia, Nigeria and Ukraine. One of the IMF's recent proposals is a more unified approach to dealing with state lenders that is "acceptable to Paris Club members and others" (i.e. China). These lenders also need to be treated in the same way as commercial creditors, and creditors must declare legitimate debts to avoid the problem of undisclosed loans that has plagued Zambia's neighbour Mozambique, for example.

What are the prospects for the internationalisation of the renminbi?

What, in conclusion, are the prospects for renminbi internationalisation? Capital controls have increased rather than slowed in 2020, which shows how cautious the Chinese government still is in pursuing the path of internationalisation by relaxing control. This is partly due to technical factors, but also to political considerations.

A decade ago, when the Chinese leadership began implementing extraordinary plans to internationalise the renminbi, Beijing's motivation was a disillusioned reaction to the 2008 financial crisis, which had shown the weakness of the dollar-based system. At that time, China was dangerously exposed to dollar volatility, as most of its liabilities were in dollars, while most of its assets were in renminbi. If the Chinese currency had achieved wide international use, this imbalance could have been mitigated. Therefore, influential economists and officials proposed freeing up the circulation of local currency to stimulate domestic financial liberalisation, as implemented by other major countries in the past.

Since then, China has created a market-driven offshore renminbi, set up trading centres around the world with banks designated to conduct business, and made a special effort to build such centres in Hong Kong and London. In three years, the number of banks conducting renminbi transactions rose from 900 to 10,000. Beijing promoted the renminbi as the settlement currency for China's trade, leading to significant savings for companies like Samsung which no longer needed to exchange renminbi for dollars.

Chinese leaders made it easier for companies with multiple branches to consolidate their accounts. They created an international free trade zone in Shanghai as a precursor to broader domestic liberalisation in which currency trade and transactions were the main components. They announced they would slowly open access by other countries to domestic stock and bond markets and a gradual liberalisation of foreign direct investment. They decided to liberalise domestic interest rates. They promoted the renminbi as a reserve currency and convinced many countries to accept it as part of their reserves and the IMF to include the Chinese currency as a component of SDRs.

Therefore, in 2015 the trend in the use of the renminbi were particularly positive, even though they were starting at ground level. However, this trend did not hold, for several reasons. The bond market continues to be fragmented under four different regulators (the PBoC, the Chinese Securities Regulatory Commission (the body overseeing the stock market), the China Banking and Insurance Regulatory Commission (the body overseeing the banking and insurance sectors) and the State Administration of Foreign Exchange), which have often been very interventionist. Strong supervisory measures, such as those implemented in the stock market in 2015, prevent investors from predicting market performance. Moreover, China's credit needs are still mainly served by banks rather than bonds, so the bond market remains less developed than it could be.

It is true that interventions by central banks in the US and the EU influence markets more than they used to, but the political component in China remains much larger. As in Tokyo, the market for corporate control is extremely limited, which is a barrier to significant capital flows. The recent strengthening of support for central control of state-owned enterprises and consolidation of national champions goes further in this direction. The legal system is now under even tighter political control, so market participants are unsure how disputes will be resolved. Overall capital controls have been tightened rather than relaxed as expected.

The problem of opening the market, however, is not only technical. There is a widespread desire on the part of businesses and households to move their money out of China because of uncertainty regarding the conditions under which their funds can be misappropriated. The anti-corruption campaign makes businesses and wealthy people nervous: while harsh authoritarianism is often seen in the West as a symbol of stability, in China families see it as a sign of fear and uncertainty. They would therefore like to put their money in a safer place. This problem has become much more serious compared to a few years ago, and things do not seem likely to change any time soon.

Finally, the level of debt, the slowdown in previously rapid growth which was the basis of much of China's lending and the possible decrease in efficiency in the use of debt create risks for banks, making stricter financial controls necessary for prudential purposes.

All this means that the renminbi's aspirations to become an international benchmark currency will be, at best, postponed for many years. In the end, the result is paradoxical: the more China can circulate its currency abroad without reducing capital controls or relaxing tight financial market regulation, the less it needs to liberalise the currency market to internationalise the renminbi.

Bibliography

J. Aizenman, *The Impossible Trinity: From the Policy Trilemma to the Policy Quadrilemma*. Santa Cruz, University of California, 2011.

J. Aizenman, M. Chinn, H. Ito, "The 'Impossible Trinity' Hypothesis in an Era of Global Imbalances: Measurement and Testing," *Review of International Economics*, 3(21), 447-458, 2013.

A. Amighini (edited by), "China: Champion of (Which) Globalisation?," Milano, ISPI, www.ispionline.it, 2018.

A. Amighini, "China's Belt and Road: A Game Changer?," Milano, ISPI, www.ispionline.it, 2017.

L.E. Armijo, S.N. Katada, *The Financial Statecraft of Emerging Powers*, Basingstoke, Palgrave Macmillan, 2014.

B. Bernanke, "A Fresh Approach to Fiscal Stimulus Is China's Only Solution to the Impossible Trinity Devaluations and Capital Controls Won't Work," *Bloomberg*, www.bloomberg.com, 9 March 2016.

D. Bräutigam, K.P. Gallagher, "Bartering Globalization: China's Commodity-backed Finance in Africa and Latin America," *Global Policy*, 5(3), 2014.

C.C.H. Chen, "ASEAN Financial Integration and the Belt and Road Initiative: Legal Challenges and Opportunities for China in Southeast Asia" in Z. Yun (edited by), *International Governance and the Rule of Law in China Under the Belt and Road Initiative*, Cambridge, Cambridge University Press, 2018.

X.L. Chen, Y-W. Cheung, "Renminbi Going Global," *China & World Economy*, 19(2), 2011.

Y-W. Cheung, G.N. Ma, R.N. McCauley, "Renminbising China's Foreign Assets," *Pacific Economic Review*, 16(1), 2011.

J. Chien, D. Randall, "Key Lessons for Policymakers from China's Financial Inclusion Experience," The World Bank, blogs.worldbank.org, 2018.

B.J. Cohen, *Currency Power: Understanding Monetary Rivalry*, Princeton, Princeton University Press, 2015.

S. Das, "China's Evolving Exchange Rate Regime," IMF Working Papers, www.imf.org, No. 19/50, 2019.

E. Farhi, M. Maggiori, "China versus the United States: IMS meets IPS," *American Economic Review*, 109, 2019.

J. Frankel, "China Is Not Yet Number One," *Frontiers of Economics in China*, 10(1), 2015.
A. García-Herrero, "China Cannot Finance the Belt and Road Alone," Hkust Iems Thought Leadership Briefs, www.iems.ust.hk, No. 17, 2017.
A. García-Herrero, L. Xia, "RMB Bilateral Swap Agreements: How China Chooses Its Partners?," *Asia-Pacific Journal of Accounting & Economics*, 22(4), 2015.
E.V. Gloria, "China's Exchange Rate Regimes and Their Policy Implications," Asian Center, 2014.
A. Gwiazda, "The Sluggish Internationalization of the Renminbi," *Bank i Kredyt*, 48(5), 2017.
T. Huang, "Why China Still Needs Hong Kong," Peterson Institute for International Economics, www.piie.com, 2019.
S. Horn, C.M. Reinhart, C. Trebesch, "China's Overseas Lending," NBER Working Papers, National Bureau of Economic Research, www.nber.org, 2019.
K. Johnson, "Why is China Buying Up Europe's Ports?," *Foreign Policy*, 2 February 2018.
A. Kratz, A. Feng, L. Wright, "New Data on the 'Debt Trap' Question," Rhodium Group, rhg.com, 2019.
C.H. Kuan, "Issues Facing Renminbi Internationalization: Observations from Chinese, Regional and Global Perspectives," *Public Policy Review*, 14(5), 2018.
Y. Li, "Belt and Road: A Logic Behind the Myth" in A. Amighini, *China's Belt and Road: a Game Changer?*, Milano, ISPI, www.ispionline.it, 2017.
S. Liao, D. McDowell, "Redback Rising: China's Bilateral Swap Agreements and Renminbi Internationalization," *International Studies Quarterly*, 59(3), 2015.
Z. Lin, W. Zhan, Y-W. Cheung, "China's Bilateral Currency Swap Lines," *China & World Economy*, 24(6), 2016.
C. Lo, *China's Impossible Trinity: The Structural Challenges to the "Chinese Dream"*, Basingstoke, Palgrave Macmillan, 2015.
"Vision and Actions on Jointly Building the Silk Road Economic Belt and 21st Century Maritime Silk Road," National Development Reform Commission of the PRC, 2015
"The Timing, Path, and Strategies of RMB Internationalization," People's Bank of China Study Group, 2006.
E.S. Prasad, *Gaining Currency: The Rise of the Renminbi*, New York, Oxford University Press, 2017.
E.S. Prasad, "Why China No Longer Needs Hong Kong," *The New York Times*, 3 July 2019.
C. Reinhart, C. Trebesch, "Sovereign Debt Relief and Its Aftermath," *Journal of the European Economic Association*, 14(1), 2016.

V. Shih, "Financial Instability in China: Possible Pathways and Their Likelihood," Mercator Institute for China Studies, 2017.
J. Shin, "Korea-China currency swap-financed trade settlement facility" in F. Rvekamp, H.G. Hilpert (edited by), *Currency Cooperation in East Asia*, New York, Springer, 2014.
P. Subacchi, (2017), *The People's Money*, New York, Columbia University Press, 2017.
C. Windsor, D. Halperin, "Renminbi Internationalization: Where to Next?," *Reserve Bank of Australia Bulletin*, 2018.
J. Yu, "The Belt and Road Initiative: Domestic Interests, Bureaucratic Politics and the EU-China Relations," *Asia Europe Journal*, 16, 2018.
F. Zhang, M. Yu, J. Yu, Y. Jin, "The Effect of RMB Internationalization on Belt and Road Initiative: Evidence from Bilateral Swap Agreements," *Emerging Markets Finance & Trade*, 53, 2017.
L. Zhang, K. Tao, "The Benefits and Costs of Renminbi Internationalization," ADBI Working Paper Series, No. 481, 2014.